STRANGE AND INCREDIBLE SPORTS HAPPENINGS

BY MAC DAVIS

Illustrated by Richard Powers

Cover illustration by
Richard Walz

Publishers • GROSSET & DUNLAP • New York

Foreword

This is a somewhat different kind of sports book. While certain occurrences that have taken place in the world of sports over the past century or more are duly recounted, the emphasis here is placed on aspects that include the strange, the unusual, the offbeat, the unique, and the bizarre. Thus, the tales are also unusual, in that they give us more to ponder and speculate upon than the colorless bare-bone statistics we are often left with in the record books.

The stories in this book are not critically predicated on any complete understanding of games or sports, so you need not be an inveterate fan to enjoy them. Readers of all ages who are fascinated by such diverse elements as mystery, intrigue, violence, greed, endurance, irony, and suspense (to name a few), will find themselves amused, amazed, absorbed, and perhaps even appalled at some of the entries — but primarily entertained.

Here will be found the sporting world's most baffling mysteries, its frauds, its hoaxes, its incredible records, and some of its most unbelievable victories and defeats, often decreed by a mere whim of fate. Some of these incidents and events could not have happened, **should** not have happened, with the probability of their occurrence being near-zero . . .

But they did!

1982 Printing
Library of Congress Catalog Card No. 74-27940
ISBN: 0-448-12326-6 (Paperback Edition)
ISBN: 0-448-13249-4 (Library Edition)
Copyright © 1975 by Florence Davis.
All rights reserved
Published simultaneously in Canada.
Printed in the United States of America.

Contents

	Page
Baseball's Biggest Bonehead	5
The Man They Branded a Murderer	7
The Deadliest Auto Race	8
Ice Hockey Brawls	9
A Baffling Boxing Mystery	12
The Jinx of the Middleweight Crown	15
The Peripatetic Stanley Cup	16
A Dead Heat	18
He Sat Out the World Series	20
He Forced His Way Into Infamy	21
A Farewell Party	23
The Vanished Indian	24
A Sit-Down Strike In a World Series	26
A Pennant Lost By Forfeit	27
Death in the Sky	28
Saved by an Upset	30
Baseball's Strangest Mystery	32
The Miraculous Marksman	33
A Hero's Welcome	36
The Costly Baseball Fight	39
The Hoax	39
The Michigan Assassin	42
The Exploited Giant	44
Tragedy at Indianapolis	47
The Unluckiest Ring Champion	48
The Longest Prizefight	50
The Winning Streak That Stretched to Nowhere	52
The Vanished Hockey Hero	54
Danger for the Umpire	55
Don't Hurt Mother on Mother's Day	57
The Hero Who Disappeared	59
Happy Jack's Wild Pitch	60
The Endurable Baseball Player	62
Sweet Retribution	63
A Race Horse That Changed History	67
The Pitching Feat Didn't Count	68

	Page
A Ballplayer's Nightmare	69
The Murdered Race Horse	71
A Baseball Game Without End	72
The Unluckiest World Series Pitcher	74
The Baseball Holdout With a Secret	77
The $100,000 Muff	78
The Jockey Who Came Back From the Dead	80
The Wrong Derby Winner	82
The First Man to Swim the English Channel	84
Never Give Up!	86
A Gallop to Ignomiry	86
A Broken Leg For a Football Star	88
Three Legs and Heart	91
The Wrong-Way Pep Talk	93
A Gridiron Massacre	94
A Castoff's Farewell	96
Sweet Kiss	97
Felix the Fourth	99
The First International Fist-Fight	101
The First Ladies' Day	103
The Champion and the Fly	106
It Happened on Opening Day	108
When One Strike was Out	110.
The Saga of "Good-Time Charlie"	112
Calling it Quits	114
The Olympic Champion Was an Impostor	115
"Mama's Boy"	118
The No-Hit Game That Didn't Count	120
An Unforgettable Thanksgiving Day	122
A Heaven-to-Earth Catch of a Baseball	123
The Football Game That Caused a Gun Duel	124
Doomed Men of Glory	126

Baseball's Biggest Bonehead

In every baseball season a number of newcomers come to play a key role in the bitterly contested pennant races of both leagues. Some, of course, go on to become baseball greats, while others may achieve fame for other reasons.

One young rookie, in the enthusiasm and inexperience of his youth, committed such a costly mistake for his team that it branded him as baseball's biggest bonehead. That luckless young rookie was Fred Merkle.

He was barely past 18 when he came on the scene to play for the old New York Giants as a first baseman. He was considered a sensational newcomer of great promise.

In the 1908 pennant campaign, the Giants and the Chicago Cubs were in a fierce and close race for the National League flag. The Cubs had won this pennant two years in a row, and now wanted it for their third consecutive season. The Giants, of course, piloted by the immortal John McGraw, the toughest loser in baseball, wanted the flag for their own glory.

Late that season the Giants and the Cubs tangled in a game upon which the league lead hinged. Rookie Fred Merkle, with only about 30 major-league games behind him, was playing first base for the Giants on that all-important September afternoon. It was a hard-fought game. But in the last half of the ninth inning, with the score tied, 1 to 1, and two outs, and with a Giant runner on first, rookie Fred Merkle hit a long single, advancing the runner to third. The next hitter also singled, and the runner on third apparently scored the winning run to end the game with a Giant victory. But, instead of running to second base while the winning run was crossing home plate, Merkle broke for the clubhouse.

The alert Cub second baseman saw the rookie's mistake. He called for the ball, touched second, and then claimed that the winning run didn't count because of Fred Merkle's failure to touch second base.

Although more than 20,000 fans had witnessed the costly mistake, no two of them saw it the same way. It caused such a commotion, so much confusion, and touched off such a riotous demonstration on the playing field that the umpire ruled the game a tie. It took 24 hours before an official decision was handed down. The game was ordered to be replayed at a later date.

Overnight, the 18-year-old Merkle became the unhappiest and most heartbroken newcomer in baseball. Even more tragically, he was thoughtlessly and cruelly branded as its biggest bonehead.

Because of that disputed game, the regular season closed with the Giants and Cubs deadlocked for first place. A playoff was necessary to decide the pennant. The Cubs eventually won the playoff and became National League champions for their third successive year.

When it happened, Fred Merkle, whose failure to touch second had cost the coveted prize for the Giants, came to manager McGraw and weepingly said: "I've lost a pennant for you, Mr. McGraw. You'd better fire me before I make another bonehead mistake."

And the toughest loser in baseball growled back at the penitent player: "Fire you! Forget it, son! I could use a carload of ballplayers like you!"

Rookie Fred Merkle stayed in the majors and went on to become an outstanding first baseman for 16 seasons. But the error of his youth haunted him to the end and he never lived down the shame of his carelessness. To his last day in the majors, and for many years beyond, Fred Merkle was known as "the bonehead who forgot to touch second."

The Man They Branded a Murderer

Carl Mays was once branded a murderer and almost outlawed from baseball because he committed a crime singular in its annals. He killed a man in a major-league game.

In his time, Carl Mays was an unlikely pitcher for big-league fame. Son of a penniless preacher, he had a boyhood filled with hardships. Before he was 12, he was doing a man's work on a farm, with no time for school or play. Nevertheless, he educated himself and also learned how to pitch, and at 22 he crashed the big leagues as a hurler. He was unlike all others, because he pitched **underhand!** Carl Mays became one of the best in the game. But he also became a storm center of the majors. Controversy always raged around him.

On the afternoon of August 16, 1920, Carl Mays pitched for the New York Yankees against the pennant-bound Cleveland Indians. Up to bat came the Indians' star shortstop, Ray Chapman, a noted plate-crowder. Mays fired his speedy submarine ball, and down went Ray Chapman at home plate — with a crushed skull. Within hours, he was dead, the first and only player to be killed by a pitched ball in a major-league game.

The horror of that tragic accident shook the baseball world to its roots. Carl Mays suddenly became the most despised man in the game. Angry players and furious fans branded him a murderer, demanding that he be outlawed from baseball forever.

Silently and stoically, proud Carl Mays suffered all the violent abuse heaped upon him. Ignoring cruel taunts hurled at him from rival dugouts, and even threats against his life, he continued to pitch, completing that unhappy season with 26 victories. In further proof of his talent and guts, he won 27 games the season afterward. Although he bore the stigma of a murderer for the rest of his pitching days, Carl Mays completed his tumultuous career in the majors with more than 200 hurling victories.

The Deadliest Auto Race

In 1903, all Europe was agog over the auto race from Paris to Madrid that covered a distance of 870 miles. The race had drawn 216 top drivers to compete for the auto racing championship of the world.

Thousands upon thousands of curious onlookers had lined the dirt roads to watch the newfangled gasoline buggies speed by. The race started as a gala affair with a carnival atmosphere. But, soon enough, the event turned into the bloodiest nightmare imaginable.

In their excitement, spectators refused to stay off the roads and out of the way of speeding cars. As a result, many drivers lost control of their cars and plunged into the crowds, killing not only themselves, but spectators by the scores.

Finally, when the drivers had covered only 343 miles, police officials called a halt to the race at Bordeaux.

Calculating time, distance and casualties, that automobile race had cost a life-and-a-half for every mile. An unbelievable total of 550 people were killed by the automobiles, and hundreds more were injured. It was, in truth, the most horrifying and tragic sports event in history.

Ice Hockey Brawls

As ice hockey increases in popularity, it seems that the number of brawls on the ice also increases. Fines against players are sometimes imposed as a disciplinary punishment after such wild and furious action takes place. In more than half a century of National Hockey League competition, however, some frightening dramas of violence have been produced.

Curiously, some of hockey's immortal players have precipitated the most violent of these brawls. Back in 1955, the legendary Maurice ("Rocket") Richard, the captain of the Montreal Canadiens, was the greatest star in the game. One night, in a game against the Boston Bruins, he became involved in a rumble with some tough Bruins, and during that slugfest was cracked on the head with a hockey stick. "The Rocket" really lost his temper; without much ado, he swung his stick and likewise cracked the head of the nearest rival player. Then he attacked another player, breaking his stick over his head. When an official tried to stop the enraged "Rocket" on his heedless onslaught, Richard slugged the referee. Before he was dragged off the ice, he left behind him almost half-a-dozen blood-stained and battered rival players. Police were called in to restore a semblance of order.

That brawl precipitated a frightening aftermath. When Maurice Richard was fined and suspended for the balance of that season, more than 30,000 of his frenzied admirers went berserk on the streets of Montreal, and for more than seven hours engaged in a terrifying outbreak of violence and property destruction, creating one of the costliest mob riots in Canadian history.

Perhaps the most unforgettable tussle was precipitated by the National Hockey League's all-time bad man, the immortal Eddie Shore. In a game on December 12, 1933, between the Boston Bruins and the Toronto Maple Leafs, "Blood-and-Guts" Eddie knocked down Toronto's star forward, Ace Bailey, with such savage force that Bailey crashed to the ice with a fractured skull. It touched off the longest ice brawl in the League's history. Fists and sticks laid low many players. The battle royal lasted almost an hour before police stopped it. Both Ace Bailey and Eddie Shore wound up in a hospital. When Ace Bailey recovered, he had a silver plate in his head and never played hockey again.

After that memorable free-for-all, the legendary Eddie Shore was almost outlawed from the National Hockey League. There was an ironic end to that most

violent of all ice melees. Soon after Ace Bailey came out of the hospital, some of the most famous hockey players came to Toronto to play a benefit game in order to raise money for the injured hockey star. One of the players was Eddie Shore, the man who had almost killed him.

Before that particular game began, Ace Bailey walked to the center of the rink, shook hands with Eddie Shore, and said loudly and clearly for the hushed thousands of fans jamming the arena, "I hold no grudge against Eddie Shore. He is the most vicious player who ever lived, but he is also the cleanest player I've ever faced. What happened to me is all part of this game. I hold no grudge against Eddie Shore."

Then Ace Bailey and Eddie Shore embraced, and walked off the ice, hand in hand, as friends.

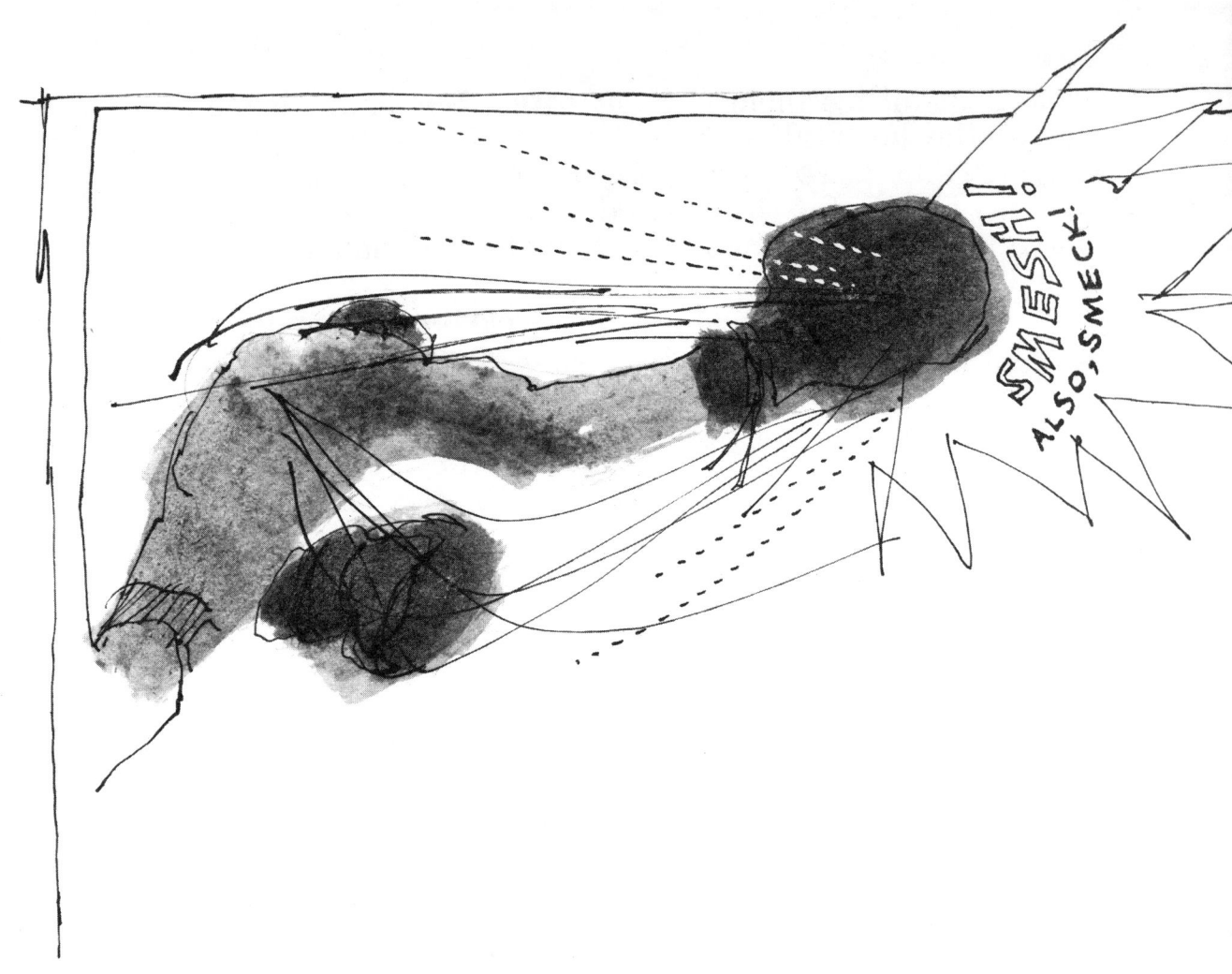

A Baffling Boxing Mystery

In the annals of boxing there have been only brief reigns for some champions. The world champion whose reign was perhaps the shortest of all was the one-time light-heavyweight boxer known as Battling Siki.

Louis Phal (his true name) began as an unwanted homeless boy in the deep obscurity of Senegal, in West French Africa. There, one day, he was found starving by a famous German ballerina who took pity on him and brought him to Paris. Eventually, he was adopted by a French family. Although he spoke only his tribal language at first, he eventually learned to speak French, and also a couple of other languages.

As time went by and Louis Phal grew older, he

became restless in his quiet life, and drifted into professional fighting. He changed his name to Battling Siki. For a time, he remained a fistic nobody. In 1922, however, a kind Fate smiled upon him. Overnight he was lifted out of obscurity and catapulted into world fame.

In September of that year Battling Siki crawled into a ring to do battle against France's fabulous "Orchid Man" and World War I hero, Georges Carpentier, the most famous prizefighter France ever had. At that time, Georges Carpentier was the world's light-heavyweight boxing champion — a fistic idol for the whole world to admire.

Georges Carpentier had taken on the unknown Battling Siki in a championship bout for his light-heavyweight title merely to entertain a legion of admirers who worshipped at his shrine. The odds on world champion Georges Carpentier to flatten Battling Siki in a few rounds were about 50 to 1, at least.

But on that memorable night of September 24, 1922, in Paris, perhaps the biggest upset in fistic history took place. Battling Siki destroyed the handsome "Orchid Man" in only six rounds and left him senseless on the ring-floor. He became the new world's light-heavyweight champion.

Overnight, Battling Siki became the new fistic celebrity of the Parisian boulevards and played that role to the hilt. His high living, nightly champagne parties, and bizarre capers made headlines throughout the world. Dressed in the height of fashion, Battling Siki often paraded the streets of Paris leading a lion on a leash.

But only a few months after winning the world's light-heavyweight championship, Battling Siki found himself badly strapped for spending money. He was inveigled into going to Ireland to defend his 175-pound world title against the famed American-Irish boxing master, Mike McTigue, for a purse of only ten thousand dollars.

What's more, Battling Siki agreed to defend his title against the popular Irishman in Dublin on St. Patrick's Day of 1923.

Before a wildly partisan crowd of more than 50,000 Irishmen rooting for Mike McTigue, champion Battling Siki went 20 furious rounds to a referee's decision. Naturally, the Irish referee gave the decision — a most questionable one — to Mike McTigue, who thus became the new light-heavyweight champion.

After a reign of only five months, Battling Siki was dethroned. It was perhaps the shortest reign of any world boxing champion.

Two years later, Battling Siki came to the United States in an attempt to reclaim his lost world title. But on the night of December 14, 1925, his lifeless body was found in the gutter of a rain-swept street. He had been shot in the back. The mysterious murder of the 28-year-old Battling Siki was never solved. It still haunts sports memory.

The Jinx of the Middleweight Crown

Ever since the middleweight boxing division came into existence in 1884, a strange jinx has plagued most of the fist-fighters who have been lucky and capable enough to capture the world's middleweight title. No other boxing title — from flyweight to heavyweight — has been so bewitched and plagued as the middleweight crown. Few of the champs of the 160-pound boxing division have escaped its ill effects.

The jinx revealed itself with the first recognized world's middleweight champion — the original Jack Dempsey ("The Nonpareil"), a fabulous middleweight-great. Widespread was his fame, and huge was his ring fortune. Upon the loss of his middleweight crown, however, he wound up broke, friendless, forsaken, and in shattered health. When he died, he was buried in an unmarked grave.

For a time, the legendary Kid McCoy, as deserving a ring warrior as ever lived, wore the world's middleweight crown. The jinx worked on him, too. He murdered his sweetheart in a jealous rage and went to prison for 20 years. When he came out, lonely, bitter and forsaken, he took his own life.

Billy Papke was once the world's middleweight champion. He, too, fell under the wicked spell of the middleweight-jinx. He killed himself.

Harry Greb, the "Pittsburgh Windmill," was perhaps the most amazing of all middleweight champions, engaging in more than 400 bouts, even though he went blind in one eye. While still in his early 30's, he went into a hospital for some minor surgery on his nose — and died on the operating table.

Mickey Walker, the "Toy Bulldog" of the ring, was a most unusual world's middleweight champ in his time. He made millions, but wound up broke.

Tiger Flowers won fame as the first black fighter to capture the world's middleweight title, but he also fell victim to the omnipotent jinx. He died while undergoing some minor eye surgery.

Vince Dundee was one of the toughest men ever to wear the 160-pound crown. But while still young, he died of a mysterious disease which had turned his powerful body to stone.

No champion was more glamorous than Marcel Cerdan, the Frenchman who captured the middleweight title in 1948. But he was killed in a plane crash soon after.

Back in the 50's, the Englishman Randy Turpin surprised the boxing world by licking Sugar Ray Robinson and winning the world's middleweight title. But, in time, Randy Turpin also fell victim. He committed suicide.

So it has been over the years with many of the fighters who once won the world's middleweight boxing crown. Indeed, no other ring title has been so bewitched. Unquestionably, it's the weirdest jinx in the sports world.

The Peripatetic Stanley Cup

The Stanley Cup, National Hockey League's most prized trophy, is awarded annually to the world-champion hockey team. It came into existence in 1893 when the Governor-General of Canada, Frederick Arthur, Lord Stanley of Preston, purchased it for less than forty-eight dollars. He then donated it as a special prize for the best hockey team extant. Winning the Stanley Cup is a professional team's outstanding achievement of the year. Strangely, this treasured trophy, which cost so little and survives as North America's oldest sports award, has had a curious history.

Over the years, several attempts were made to steal the famed Cup.

Once, a star player who had been given the honor of carrying the Stanley Cup to a victory banquet suddenly went berserk and kicked the silver trophy into the Rideau Canal in Ottawa. Fortunately, the canal was frozen over at the time, so the Stanley Cup wasn't lost forever. It was recovered slightly damaged.

Another time, the Cup was carelessly abandoned on a street corner by a player who had charge of it. It wasn't retrieved for many hours.

Still another time, an irate club owner thought so little of the Stanley Cup in his possession that he had to be restrained from throwing it into a lake.

Once, the players of a world-championship hockey team arrived with the Stanley Cup at a photographer's studio to pose for some special pictures. When that was done, they left the studio but forgot to take the Stanley Cup with them. It was months before the abandoned trophy was recovered from the studio basement.

Believe it or not, the coveted Stanley Cup was once left with an elderly lady who knew nothing of its prestigious value, and for a time, she used it as a flower pot.

And, another time, the Stanley Cup was also used as a chamber pot.

Once, a hockey team lost possession of the famed trophy when it was beaten in the Stanley Cup series, but the players refused to turn it over to the victors until they had had a riotous celebration of their own. So, winner and loser of the Stanley Cup engaged in a wild and fierce brawl for its possession.

Not too long ago, a thief broke into Hockey's Hall of Fame and stole the Stanley Cup. What he didn't know when he pulled off the robbery was that the Stanley Cup he filched was only a duplicate of the original. Some years ago a Danish silversmith created the replica which could be used for ceremonial purposes. That was the actual trophy taken by the invader.

Months later, the missing duplicate appeared as mysteriously as it had been stolen on the doorstep of a Toronto police constable.

Now the original Stanley Cup is safely ensconced in Hockey's Hall of Fame, as is its duplicate, awaiting to be awarded to the world-champion team when the National Hockey League campaign reaches its climax with post-season play-offs each year.

A Dead Heat

There have been many famous dead heats in horse racing, but the most fantastic race of all took place at old Gravesend, New York, in the summer of 1873.

In that race, a five-year-old horse named Bing Aman finished in a dead heat with a horse named Mart Jordan. The two horses were sent to the post to run again on that simmering summer day.

Again they finished together. They were sent back to the post for the third time.

And a third time, they finished in a dead heat!

The owners of both horses were stubborn. For a fourth time, the two steeds were sent to the post to race over the one-and-three-quarter-mile track.

And again, they seemed to finish in a dead heat, although the judges declared Bing Aman winner by a nose. The payoff was that the spectators refused to accept the judging and rioted, almost destroying the race track.

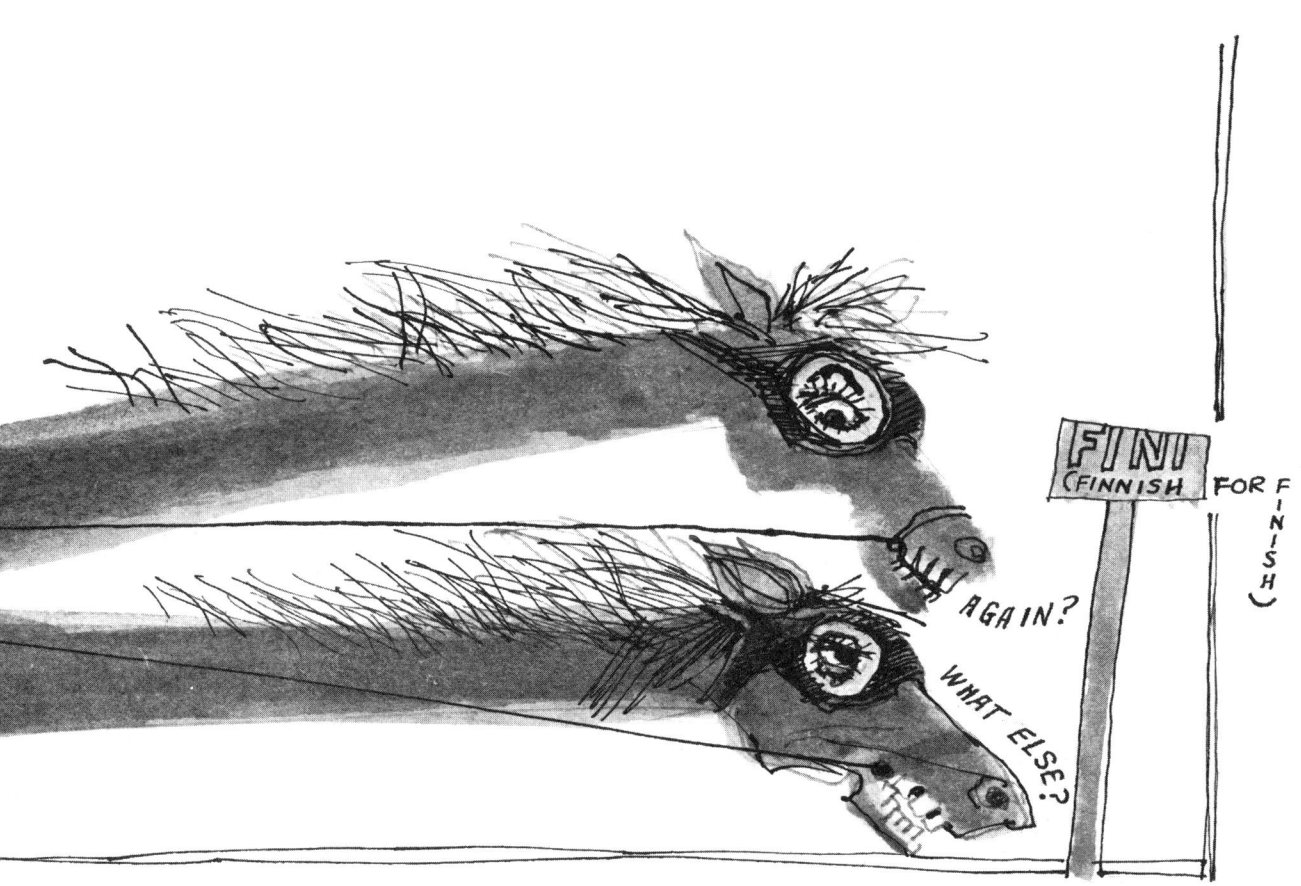

He Sat Out the World Series

The goal of every major-league manager is to win a pennant, so it's an unwise pilot who does not go into a World Series with his best players. But strange as it may be, there was once a pennant-winning manager who deliberately refused to use his star player in the post-season classic. The manager was Donnie Bush. The player who didn't play was Hazen ("Kiki") Cuyler.

In 1927, Donnie Bush, a once-famous shortstop, was manager of the Pittsburgh Pirates. It was his first season, and he astonished the baseball world by piloting his team to a pennant.

That glorious season, manager Bush had a fleet-footed outfielder who could run like a man pursued by demons, throw as if his arm were a slingshot, and hit around .350! He was Kiki Cuyler, who played in the majors for eighteen seasons. Cuyler, only 25, was already a World Series hero of renown; his magnificent playing two seasons earlier had helped clinch the baseball championship for the Pirates. He was expected to shine brilliantly in the 1927 World Series.

However, Cuyler was a superstitious player, and Donnie Bush was a stubborn pilot. Hence, a bitter feud developed between the two men that was to prove costly.

Kiki Cuyler had always batted number three in the Pirates' lineup. Superstitiously, what he feared most was to bat number two. But shortly before the 1927 World Series, manager Bush juggled his lineup and moved Cuyler from the three spot to number two.

"Don't do it, skipper!" Cuyler pleaded. "Don't put me in that number two spot. It's a jinx for me!"

"Ridiculous!" snorted Bush. "You're hitting over .330 now and it won't make any difference to you. I want you to bat where I put you!"

Kiki Cuyler refused to shift — so manager Bush benched him.

Then came the World Series against the formidable New York Yankees, at which time Pirate manager Donnie Bush became even more unyielding. He not only wanted his star outfielder to bat in the number two spot, but he wanted Kiki to say he would hit second in the lineup and like it!

Kiki Cuyler was willing to play in the Series, and even bat number two, but he refused to tell his manager that he would like it. So Donnie Bush nursed a grudge, and kept the Pirates' star player and best hitter sitting on the bench.

With Kiki Cuyler forced to sit out the Series, the Pittsburgh team went down to a most humiliating defeat — in four straight games!

It was the only time in history that a famous available ballplayer unwillingly sat out an entire World Series because his manager stubbornly and foolishly held a grudge against him!

Kiki Cuyler never again played for the Pittsburgh Pirates after that disastrous defeat that year, but curiously enough, two seasons later, he sparked the Chicago Cubs to a pennant, and then, three seasons after that, once again. From each of those two post-season October classics, Kiki Cuyler emerged an outstanding World Series hero, and eventually entered baseball's Hall of Fame.

He Forced His Way Into Infamy

In the history of the major leagues, there are many stories of ballplayers who aggressively muscled their way to fame, but only Fred McMullin forced himself into everlasting infamy. In the five seasons he toiled for the Chicago White Sox, he was a utility second or third baseman, but he never even once tasted the glory of hitting .300. As a major-leaguer, Fred McMullin was practically a nobody.

In the 1919 pennant campaign, his good fortune was to be a utility infielder for the Chicago White Sox, then hailed as the most fabulous team in the game.

One late September afternoon, shortly before the season ran out, with the White Sox already an easy pennant winner, Fred McMullin was sitting in a hidden corner of the locker room soaking an injured ankle in a tub of hot water.

Unaware of his presence, two White Sox teammates entered the seemingly deserted locker room to engage in a whispered conversation. Listening carefully, Fred McMullin overheard them discussing details of a plan in which they were going to make a "financial killing" on the forthcoming World Series.

Fred McMullin hobbled out to confront the two conspirators, and to their amazement, he demanded to be "let in on the scheme" so that he also could make a few easy bucks for himself. Otherwise, he threatened, he would tell what he had heard.

Trapped, the two players agreed to include Fred McMullin in their plot to "clean up" on the World Series. McMullin, happily satisfied, believed that by his cleverness he had come into "a good thing" with some of his teammates. But little did Fred McMullin realize just what he had muscled his way into.

A couple of days later, when more specific arrangements were revealed to him, Fred McMullin discovered that he had become involved in a gambling plot to "throw the 1919 World Series" against the Cincinnati Reds. His partners in crime were such White Sox stars as the fabulous pitcher Eddie Cicotte, brilliant hurler Claude Williams, outfielder Happy Felsch, first baseman Chick Gandil, third baseman Buck Weaver, shortstop Swede Risberg, and the incomparable outfielder, "Shoeless" Joe Jackson.

Fred McMullin contributed nothing to the "success" of the evil plot that almost destroyed major-league baseball. He appeared in only two games in the World Series (which was duly lost by the Chicago White Sox), and each time only as a pinch hitter. But in September of 1920, when the scandal of the "thrown World Series" broke and became public knowledge, Fred McMullin shared the full fate of the other seven players involved in that evil conspiracy. Like the others, he was driven from the majors in shame and exiled from organized baseball for life!

A Farewell Party

Early each year, big-league baseball players take off on a happy journey to warmth and sunshine for their annual pilgrimage to the spring training camps. "Send-off parties" are often given by home-town folks and friends at that time. The once-famous pitcher, Walter ("Big Ed") Morris, starred in one of the most shocking of these "farewell parties."

Big Ed Morris was a happy-go-lucky pitcher out of Alabama who came up to the big leagues with the Chicago Cubs in 1922. But his first bid for fame and fortune was a flop! He couldn't win a game all season, and it so discouraged him that he quickly disappeared from the majors. He wasn't heard of again for six years.

When Big Ed was crowding 30, he showed up in the spring training camp of the Boston Red Sox, and this time he made the grade. He became one of the most sensational pitchers in the majors. In his rookie season, although the Red Sox wound up in last place, he won 19 games!

In February of 1932, Big Ed could hardly wait for the annual call to spring training camp. He was impatient to be off and to work himself into shape for the new baseball season. His friends insisted on giving him a farewell party before he left, and in grateful appreciation, pitcher Big Ed Morris consented to linger on for an extra few days so that he would be guest of honor.

It was held on February 29th. His friends had arranged a fish-fry party, and everybody was having a good time — but most of all, Big Ed Morris. Then, while the party was in full swing, the famous pitcher became embroiled in a friendly argument with one of the guests. Too soon, it turned into a bitter quarrel — and suddenly, it ended in violence. Before the eyes of the horrified guests and all his friends, Big Ed Morris was stabbed to death!

It was an ironic and tragic finish to the career of a famous pitcher who was on his way to spring training camp but never reached it — because he was murdered at the "send-off-party" given in his honor.

The Vanished Indian

Louis Sockalexis was the first Indian to play in baseball's major leagues. In his time, he was so exceptional that he grew in popular imagination as a mythical figure. Although he played only three seasons, he was acclaimed as one of the greatest players ever.

Sockalexis left the Penobscot Indian reservation to become a baseball star at Holy Cross College. Six feet tall, 190 pounds heavy, he was as handsome as a man ever was, and as graceful and fast as a race horse. Before the turn of the century, he ran a hundred yards in

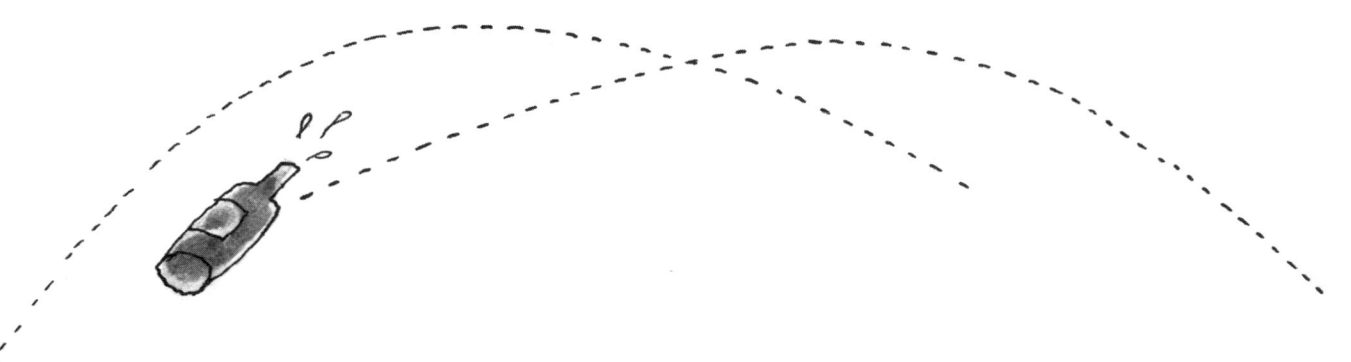

under ten seconds. When Sockalexis played one season in the old Knox County League in Maine, his feats were so heroic that he inspired the manager of one of the clubs in that league to write stories for boys and use him as a model for the fictitious character he created, "Frank Merriwell." The Frank Merriwell series books that evolved delighted, awed, and inspired millions of boys for decades.

Sockalexis crashed the major leagues in 1897, when he became an outfielder for the Cleveland club, then known as the Spiders. So dominant was his playing and influence that the Cleveland team became known as the Cleveland Indians.

But the white man's temptations caused the downfall of Sockalexis. At a party, his teammates persuaded him to taste his first strong drink. It sealed his fate as a ballplayer. Thereafter, he couldn't stay away from whiskey — and before long, he became a hopeless drunkard.

After only three seasons, Sockalexis drank himself out of the majors. Eventually, he sank deeper into degradation, and wound up a forsaken and shabby beggar. In time, he drifted back to the Penobscot Indian reservation from whence he came, and there he lived in despair and oblivion, until December 24, 1913, when he died at only forty-two.

A Sit-Down Strike
In a World Series

In 1918, big-league baseball was in bad shape. The world was at war, and many players were in military service. Nevertheless, the pennant campaign went on in both major leagues, until the ruling powers of the game ordered that the season be brought to an end on September 1. On Labor Day, that year, the Chicago Cubs won the flag in the National League, and the Boston Red Sox captured the pennant in the American League.

The two pennant winners of that short season clashed in a World Series that started on September 5 and ended by September 11. It was a classic with a completely unexpected twist.

At the end of four games played, the two teams were deadlocked. Each club had won twice. The players were disgruntled and unhappy, because the games had been washouts at the gate, and they realized that they would wind up with little money for their share of the World Series jackpot.

A couple of hours before it was time to play the fifth game, all of the players staged a sit-down strike. They simply refused to play until they were promised a larger portion of the receipts.

For more than an hour a strike committee representing the players argued with the club owners and the presidents of both leagues, while thousands of fans in the ballpark yelled impatiently for the game to begin. Finally, the striking players were persuaded to be loyal to their club, the public, and the game itself, by giving up their stubborn demands for a larger cut. The rebellious players suited up and went out to play. Ultimately, the Boston Red Sox won the championship, four games to two.

The winning Red Sox players received $1,108.45 each, while the losing Chicago Cub players received $671.00 each. It was the poorest of World Series payoffs.

A Pennant Lost By Forfeit

On September 7, 1889, the final day of the baseball season, when the old Brooklyn Dodgers and the St. Louis team were locked in a tie for the pennant, a large crowd of frenzied fans packed the ballpark to witness the deciding contest.

The St. Louis team jumped into an early lead and for seven innings sat on top of a score of four runs to two. Victory seemed certain for St. Louis as the eighth inning began. But then the sky clouded and a creeping darkness enveloped the field. The St. Louis players began to clamor for the umpire to call the game on account of darkness. The Dodgers were equally vociferous in demanding that the game be continued, even though it had become too dark to play.

For his part, the umpire seemed to be in no hurry to stop the contest. There were only two more innings to play. He ordered that the game be continued. Whereupon the St. Louis third baseman, Arlie Latham, a renowned diamond clown, decided to force the issue. He requested the bat boy to bring out a dozen large candles, and when he had them, he lined them up in front of the St. Louis dugout and lit them.

The crowd laughed uproariously at that pointed hint to the stubborn umpire. Annoyed and embarrassed, the umpire walked over and blew out the candles, but no sooner had he returned to his position than Arlie Latham again lit them. Once more the umpire came over and blew out the candles — and again Arlie Latham lit them. The puffing umpire, who was not amused, blew them out once more. He sternly warned the St. Louis players to "cut out the comedy" and get on with the game. Not one to give up so easily, Arlie Latham sneaked out of the dugout and lit the candles a fourth time.

It was then that the umpire, in a bellow heard all over the ballpark, announced that the Dodgers were the winners by a forfeit score of 9-0.

A free-for-all followed. But the decision stood, and

the Brooklyn Dodgers, even though they had been trailing by a score of 4-2 when the game was stopped, captured the deciding game for the pennant by virtue of a forfeit.

Thus it happened once in baseball history that a team lost a championship flag because of twelve candles.

Death in the Sky

When outfielder Len Koenecke first arrived in the major leagues, back in 1932, he was a sensational rookie for headline fame. The New York Giants had paid the then-unheard-of price of $100,000 to acquire him from a minor-league club. As it turned out, however, Koenecke didn't play for the Giants for long, because he was an irresponsible, wild-living ballplayer who exhausted the manager's patience with bizarre antics on and off the diamond. The Giants got rid of their expensive rookie after only forty-two games.

Len Koenecke vanished from the major leagues, and wasn't seen there again until 1934, when he showed up on the roster of the former Brooklyn Dodgers. This time out, he was a full-season asset. He starred in all the scheduled games, fielded his outfield position flawlessly, and batted a rousing .320.

But the following season, Len Koenecke again turned into a most difficult ballplayer to control. Fabled Casey Stengel, then the pilot of the Dodgers, was hard pressed to keep him out of mischief. Stengel eventually tired of tolerating Koenecke's erratic behavior, and on the afternoon of September 17th of that 1935 season, when the Dodgers were playing a series in St. Louis against the Cardinals, outfielder Len Koenecke was informed that he was no longer wanted, and he was ordered to pack up.

Seething mad, Koenecke promptly booked flight passage on a commercial plane for his return home. Enroute, ballplayer Len Koenecke created such a dis-

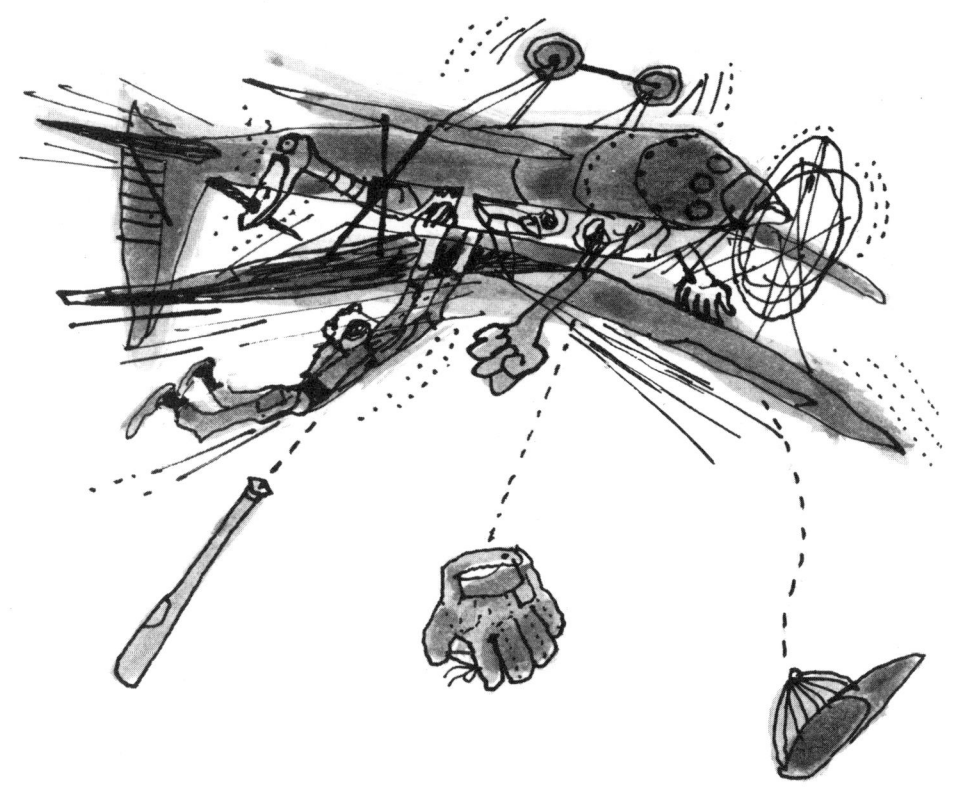

turbance that when the plane made a brief stop, he was again discharged — physically.

Now wild with rage, the outfielder lost no time chartering a private plane to continue his journey homeward. When it took off, only three people were aboard — the pilot, a co-pilot, and Len Koenecke.

For a while, the angry ballplayer just sat in his seat and sulked. But when the plane was flying over Toronto, Koenecke went berserk and tried to seize the controls. The pilot and co-pilot fought him off to keep the plane from crashing. It became a fierce and desperate brawl, fought with three lives at stake, and finally ended with Koenecke literally clubbed to death.

In the trial that followed to weigh all evidence connected with the tragedy, the pilot and co-pilot were exonerated on grounds of self-defense.

On that September day of 1935, when death came to Len Koenecke while flying high in the sky, he was only 28 years old.

Saved By an Upset

Over the football years, many hard-to-believe upsets have taken place to flavor gridiron history with the unexpected. The victims sometimes paid a costly price for their downfall. But a startling upset once paid off with a strange reward for the losers. It happened in 1942.

In that season, Boston College came up with more than just a powerful winning football team; it was the outstanding team in college football, a mighty powerhouse that roared through its schedule crushing all grid-opponents by lopsided scores. When it came to its final game of that season, the undefeated team, rich with a flock of All-America stars in its lineup, not only had the national collegiate football championship almost clinched, but it also was Rose Bowl bound.

The final game to complete an undefeated season was a mere formality. It was against Boston's tradi-

tional rival, Holy Cross, a weak team that had been able to win only four games during the season. Boston was expected to overwhelm Holy Cross by at least half a dozen touchdowns.

But, as sometimes happens in football play, when least expected, a miracle came to pass. In that game, everything went wrong for heavily favored and undefeated Boston college, and everything went just right for underdog and oft-beaten Holy Cross. The mighty Boston College team went down to a crushing defeat by a lopsided score of 55 to 12. It was one of the most unforgettable upsets in college football history!

For Boston College, that unbelievable upset was more than a dent in its gridiron prestige. The loss tumbled the Boston team from its glory heights and shattered its claim to a national football championship.

No wonder none of its players had the desire to attend a celebration which had been planned for that night to mark the completion of a glorious and undefeated season. The party was to be held at a well-known nightclub, the Cocoanut Grove.

But following the upset, all the Boston College football players begged off attending it. The dejected teammates sneaked off to their homes, there to hide from everyone who had seen their downfall and to stew in the bitterness of their disappointment. Naturally, the celebration party was called off.

The next day all the unhappy players of the beaten Boston College team discovered that the upset which had destroyed their glory for a football championship had been a blessing in disguise. The upset had rewarded them with their lives!

The night before, the Cocoanut Grove, at the height of its festivities, was swept by a sudden fire, and more than 400 people partying there lost their lives in a fiery holocaust. But not one Boston College football player who would otherwise have been there was a victim of that tragedy.

Yes, over the years, there have been many upsets. But the upset of the 1942 season that befell the undefeated Boston College football team had its compensation for both sides.

Baseball's Strangest Mystery

One of baseball's greatest players is the star in baseball's strangest mystery.

In his time, handsome, colorful Edward J. Delahanty was an outstanding star in the major leagues. An incomparable first baseman, he was also one of baseball's mightiest sluggers. In the era of the "dead ball" he hit .400 twice. His batting average for 16 years in the majors was .346. "Big Ed" also achieved the unique distinction of being the only player ever to win the batting championship of both major leagues. In 1899, while playing with the Philadelphia Phillies, he won the National League bat crown with a .408 batting mark. And in 1902, while playing with the Washington Senators, he hit .376 to win the American League batting championship.

Fabulous ballplayer that he was, Ed Delahanty was also baseball's most magnificent roughneck. A handsome, happy-go-lucky man with a taste for excitement, he was constantly in debt, always in some trouble with women, and ready for the wildest capers.

On June 25, 1903, while he was still at the height of his fame as baseball's most glamorous ballplayer and hitting a robust .338 for the Washington Senators, Delahanty became so unmanageable in Detroit in a game against the Tigers that the Senators' pilot suspended him. It caused the wild Irishman to go haywire. He promptly deserted the team, wired his wife to meet him, and caught a train bound for New York.

On board, drinking heavily and causing a noisy commotion, Ed Delahanty was last seen around midnight. When the train arrived at its destination, however, the famous ballplayer was no longer on it.

Several confused stories were told to explain his strange disappearance. It was said that when the train had stopped for a few moments at Fort Erie, Ontario, at the Canadian end of the International Bridge, several annoyed conductors had ganged up on the boisterous ballplayer and tossed him off the train. But no conductor ever admitted that he had taken part in Delahanty's ejection from the train.

Another story was that Delahanty had left the train himself and started to walk across the bridge in pitch-black darkness. A watchman with a lantern appeared to warn him that the draw was open, but Delahanty had shoved the man aside and stumbled away out of sight. Likewise, no watchman was ever found who admitted seeing the famous Ed Delahanty on that fateful night.

For days, his strange disappearance mystified the sports world. On July 2nd, he was finally found. He was a corpse! His horribly mangled body was found wedged against a wharf some 20 miles below the International Bridge.

The mystery of Ed Delahanty's strange disappearance was never fully solved. Did he fall? Jump? Or was he pushed? To this day, the shocking and violent death of one of baseball's top stars has remained an unsolved mystery.

The Miraculous Marksman

Countless millions of people, down through the years, have participated in target practice, but no one has fired a rifle at a target as often and scored as many hits as did Adolph Topperwein.

Back at the turn of the century, Adolph Topperwein was something of a household word to those fascinated by precision shooting. A vaudeville performer specializing in trick shots, he toured the world giving demonstrations of his incredible marksmanship.

One day in 1906, Adolph Topperwein publicly announced that he would perform a feat never before attempted. For twelve consecutive days, for eight hours a day, he would shoot a rifle at targets, firing about every five seconds. The targets would be wooden cubes, 2½ inches square, tossed high in the air.

So it was that one December morning a huge

crowd gathered at the San Antonio Fairgrounds in Texas to watch Adolph Topperwein begin his marksmanship marathon.

On the first day, he fired at 6,500 small wooden-cube targets, and he didn't miss once!

On the second day, he fired at 6,600 more, but he missed one.

One, two, three, four, five, six, seven, and eight days, Adolph Topperwein continued shooting at his small wooden cubes every five seconds, rotating a rifle every five hundred shots. By the end of the eighth day, he had fired at 50,000 blocks thrown into the air, missing only four times!

On the ninth day of that strange marathon, Adolph Topperwein came to the firing line suffering torturous muscular cramps in his arms. He could hardly hold the rifle, but he refused to quit. For eight more hours he continued shooting at his targets. The tenth day was sheer torture, but he completed it, and also the eleventh consecutive day. He was utterly exhausted on the twelfth day, but again he remained for eight hours, firing every five seconds. At the end of that day, Adolph Topperwein collapsed from the grueling ordeal. He had shot at 72,500 targets and missed only nine!

The mark set by Adolph Topperwein in December, 1906, still stands!

A Hero's Welcome

Probably the strangest homecoming welcome for a sports hero was that given Santiago Lovell of Argentina. He was a powerfully built boxer who punched his way to glory by winning the heavyweight boxing championship in the 1932 Olympic Games held in Los Angeles. He was the only gold medal winner for the entire Argentine team, and naturally he anticipated a celebration in his honor upon his return to Buenos Aires.

It was with high hopes that the South American team boarded the ship for home, but en route something unexpected happened, and the gold medal winner became involved in an unfortunate incident. The Olympic athletes were so poorly fed and so shabbily treated aboard ship that the infuriated Santiago Lovell organized a rebellion against the authorities.

The captain of the ship called out guards to put down the insurgents, but Santiago Lovell led his teammates in a furious and bloody fist-and-club battle against the officers and guards. Finally, the mutiny was subdued and Santiago and his rioting Olympic cohorts were confined under lock and key for the rest of the voyage.

On his arrival home, instead of receiving a national welcome befitting a triumphant hero, police met the ship, and Santiago Lovell, in chains, was escorted to the nearest jail.

Later, forced to stand trial as leader of the mutiny, he was found guilty and sentenced to a brief prison term.

A Wrestler's Gold

Undoubtedly, no other sport has ever produced as many strange, weird, and comic competitors as have performed in professional wrestling. One of the weirdest of all the wrestling ancients was Yousouf, the "Terrible Turk," who wrote into wrestling history an unbelievable story far stranger than fiction.

In his time, Yousouf was a ferocious-looking giant of more than 300 pounds who came out of Turkey early in the century to amaze the world with his strength and wrestling skill. With almost ridiculous ease, he outwrestled all comers. When he came to the United States in search of greater victories and more gold, he became a sensation, not only for his professional skill, but also for his weird eccentricities. His appetite was tremendous. At one sitting, he could eat five loaves of bread, a dozen eggs, and three or four huge steaks.

Tremendous crowds flocked to see Yousouf in ring action. Wherever he wrestled, he commanded huge purses. Curiously, he always demanded that he be paid in gold. Whenever he received payment, Yousouf would stuff the gold pieces into a leather money belt which he wore strapped around his waist. Yousouf the "Terrible Turk" never lost a match.

On January 15, 1910, Yousouf went to Canada for a wrestling match in Montreal against a powerful giant known as Chaaker. It was one of the roughest and wildest wrestling bouts in history. Yousouf the "Terrible Turk" gave his opponent such a going-over that Chaaker finally collapsed, and died minutes after he had been pinned to the mat.

The tragic match prompted Yousouf to quit pro wrestling and return to his native Turkey. No amount of coaxing could induce him to remain, even though he was at the height of his fame. Yousouf stuffed all the gold he had earned on his triumphal tour into his huge money belt, strapped it tightly around his giant body, and boarded a ship for the voyage back home.

Even while on board, Yousouf the "Terrible Turk" would not remove the money belt stuffed with his fortune in gold. He locked himself in his cabin and simply refused to see anyone.

On the second day at sea, the ship ran into a violent storm. It began to sink. At the height of the panic, Yousouf suddenly appeared on deck, his money belt still strapped around his waist. He was howling with rage. He rushed to the rail and hurled himself into the turbulent sea. Although a lifeboat was nearby, the famous wrestler was unable to swim to it. The weight of his money belt, stuffed with gold pieces, quickly pulled him under. With a final horrible shriek, he disappeared beneath the waves.

Such was the ironic end of Yousouf the "Terrible Turk," a colorful wrestler who accepted payment only in gold. But the very gold he earned for his skill brought him to his untimely death.

The Costly Baseball Fight

In the last decade of the nineteenth century, the fabulous Baltimore Orioles were the tops in baseball, and their star third baseman was the pasty-faced Irishman, John J. McGraw, who also had the reputation of being the most feared brawler in the game.

On May 16, 1894, John McGraw and his Oriole teammates were in the Boston ballpark playing against the Boston club. By the middle of the game, fiery "Muggsy" McGraw had already had several verbal squabbles with some of the Boston players, and the crowd in the stands was in a frenzy.

Brawling McGraw was never a player to calm and soothe a hostile crowd, so before long, he became embroiled in a fierce fist fight with Boston's tough first baseman, Tommy "Foghorn" Tucker. While the two players fought on the field, a gang of hoodlums in the bleachers decided to add to the "fun" and confusion by setting the seats on fire. The fire spread and burned down not only the Boston ballpark, but 170 other buildings as well, causing property damage running into the millions!

The Hoax

In the early years of this century, an attractive woman suddenly popped up as a billiards player of remarkable skill. She billed herself as Miss Frances Anderson, the world's female billiards champion. Wherever she appeared to display her skill, she had a standing offer of $5,000 to wager against any woman who would compete with her. Miss Frances Anderson even played some games against top men players, and defeated them all, winning sizable wagers.

Reams of newspaper and magazine stories were written about Frances Anderson, the world's outstand-

...IF SHE HAD NICER LEGS I'D SWEAR SHE WAS MINNESOTA FATS...

ing woman billiards player. She became so famous that she also appeared on the stage (at high fees) to demonstrate her skill. She was a sensation throughout the United States, Canada, and all Europe. She even gave command performances before the crowned heads of Europe. Royalty and common folk alike fawned over her.

For almost 25 years, Frances Anderson toured the world, displaying her exceptional skill at the billiards table, and reaping a fortune in the process.

Then, one day, her singular fame suddenly exploded in a startling headline story. It revealed that Frances Anderson was really a man named Orie Anderson who had been masquerading as a female. It was the biggest and most successful hoax of its kind ever perpetrated!

When the deception was revealed, Orie Anderson quickly vanished into obscurity, never to be heard from again.

It was a long time before an embarrassed sports world forgot the male imposter who for almost a quarter of a century masqueraded as the world's foremost woman billiards player.

The Michigan Assassin

No fighter in history was linked to tragedy as much as Stanley Ketchel, the greatest middleweight champion of them all.

Born Stanislaus Kiecel on a dismal Michigan farm, he ran away from home before he was 15 to roam across the country and dwell in the jungles of hoboland. A footloose wanderer of the road, he soon became a tough, fast fist-fighter, defending himself against all the bullies of the hobo jungles in order to survive. He was no more than 17 when he became a prizefighter, simplifying his name to Stanley Ketchel, and it was immediately apparent that a new meteor was flaming across the pugilistic sky.

In the ring there were few who could withstand the savage and blazing two-fisted attack of young Ketchel. So devastating was his whirlwind onslaught that in his first 39 professional fights he quickly knocked out 35 opponents. That gave him the nickname of the "Michigan Assassin."

He was not fully 21 when, near the turn of the century, in a bloody ring battle that went 32 rounds, Stanley Ketchel became the new middleweight champion of the world.

Handsome, sprightly, and tough, the "Michigan Assassin" became the most glamorous and popular fighter of his time, a sports idol for millions of people, and also the favorite "he-man hero" of countless women. His romantic escapades made almost as many headlines as his ring victories.

Despite his fame as a middleweight king, Stanley Ketchel was doomed to misfortune. His father was murdered, and his mother was also a victim of a mysterious murder. On October 15, 1910, when Ketchel was only 24, still the invincible world's middleweight champion and a sports idol to millions, his own life came to a sudden end. While having breakfast on a lonely farm in Conway, Missouri, where he was vacationing, the famed "Michigan Assassin" ironically became victim of an assassination! He was shot and killed by a jealous farmhand named Walter Dipley, who thought that the handsome middleweight king was "trifling" with his girl friend, the ugly-duckling camp cook known as Goldie Smith. The farmhand went to prison for 23 years, and Goldie Smith vanished after that murder and was never seen again.

Born in misery, he died in tragedy, but Stanley Ketchel was one of the prize ring's truly great fighters. In 1954 his name was added to the Boxing Hall of Fame.

The Exploited Giant

Primo Carnera, a fierce-looking, snaggle-toothed giant, six-feet-six inches tall and almost 300 pounds heavy, was a strong man in an Italian circus. His place was among the freaks in a sideshow exhibit. He knew nothing about fighting with boxing gloves; nevertheless, he was persuaded to become a prizefighter.

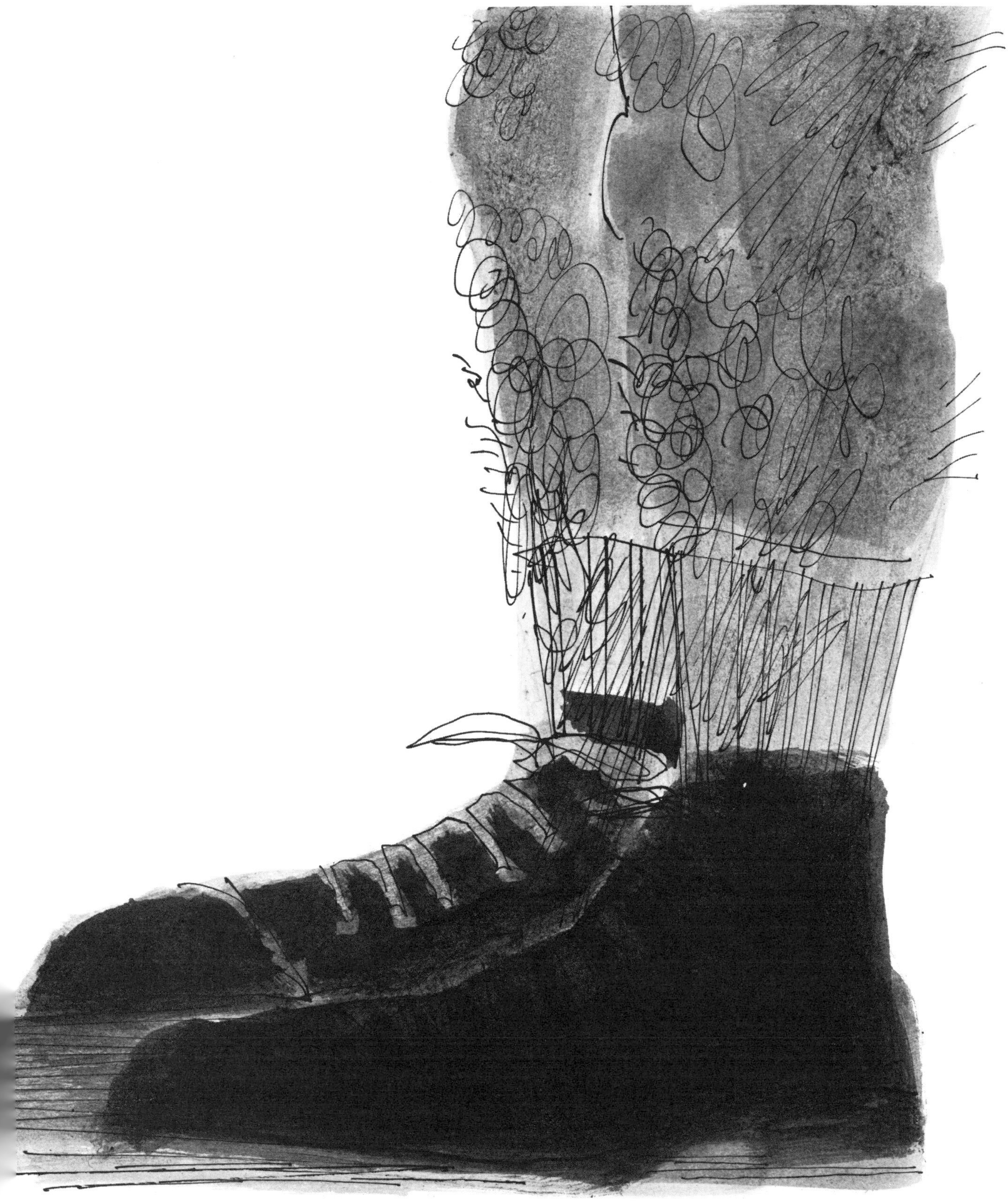

As a ring warrior, the amiable Italian was largely a pitiful joke. He couldn't hit, he had no defense, and he stumbled around the ring like a bewildered ogre. Oddly, despite his huge size, he was a timid and gentle man.

As it happened, Carnera was soon imported to the United States and taken in tow by a gang of sharpie managers whose total time behind prison bars more than equalled the Italian's twenty-four years. They planned to exploit him in a colossal fistic-sham to make a financial killing. Thus, simply by making the necessary arrangements beforehand, they saw to it that whenever Primo Carnera fought in the ring, he couldn't lose. When money wouldn't do it, threats and a display of guns and knives went a long way in convincing Carnera's opponents to "take a dive."

The gentle giant had no inkling that most of his bouts had been fixed. As a regiment of opponents fell before him, Primo Carnera began to believe that he was an invincible fighter.

To a hoodwinked public, Primo Carnera became the new heavyweight sensation of the prize ring. Although he was earning a fortune, his nefarious cohorts were picking him clean. The befuddled giant had no idea of what was going on.

One night, Primo Carnera fought a young but unwell heavyweight named Ernie Schaaf and knocked him out with a light jab. A few days later, Schaaf was dead! That tragedy was unconscionably exploited. The notoriety enabled Carnera's managers to build him up as a "killer in the prize ring" and steer him into a match for the heavyweight championship.

On the night of June 29, 1933, Primo Carnera fought the world's heavyweight champion, Jack Sharkey, and won the title by a knockout. It was a surprise to everybody — including Carnera!

Nevertheless, the Italian colossus was now the new world's heavyweight champion. His glory was brief, however. Exactly one year later, he lost the title in a fearful beating. The fistic fraud was exposed, and poor Primo Carnera was left a broken hulk. Although he had earned more than a million dollars in the ring, he had been milked dry and left penniless. He was shipped back to Italy — in effect, damaged fistic goods.

For a few years thereafter, the ex-heavyweight champion of the world was a pathetic figure, barely existing on a pittance. He was without friends, money, or hopes for the future, and yet he was still only in his twenties. Seeing that discarded, forsaken giant stirred one to pity and anger.

Eventually, Primo Carnera drifted back to the United States and became a professional wrestler. Surprisingly, he made a good living for himself, married happily, and became a naturalized citizen.

When Carnera was a prizefighter, it didn't seem possible that he would ever survive the sordid atmosphere and cruel life into which he had been innocently thrust on the basis of his monstrous size and formidable appearance. But he did! And that's what makes the Primo Carnera story so unusual.

Tragedy at Indianapolis

There have been some curious jinxes to hound sport heroes, but the hoodoo that has hounded the winners of the Indianapolis Speedway 500-mile race is now, without doubt, one of the strangest and most persistent.

The annual Indianapolis classic began in 1911, and since then, for any daredevil of the roaring road who ever gambled with his life for fame and fortune, there has been only one big goal to pursue — to win racing's Big Apple. But almost every winner of this "world series" of auto racing has been rewarded with trouble, misfortune and violent death!

One of the early winners was Gaston Chevrolet, who gave the world the now widely used Chevrolet automobile. His life ended violently when he was killed in an auto crash.

Jimmy Murphy, another early winner of the Indianapolis Grind, was also killed in an auto crash. Still another winner was Joe Boyer. He also met a violent death.

As the years passed away, so did other Indianapolis 500 champions. Slim Corum hanged himself. Frank Lockhart met a violent death, as did Ray Keech. Then came "Wild" Bill Cummings, who drove racing cars faster than any man in the world. He mocked the Grim Reaper with wild and daring bravado, and he seemed to be living under a lucky star. But soon after he won the Indianapolis 500 in record time, the jinx caught up with him, too. In an ironic twist of fate, the world's fastest auto racer was killed while driving a car on a lonely country road at only 20 miles an hour.

Then came other Indianapolis Speedway winners who added their names to the grisly roster. Floyd Roberts and George Robson met a violent death. Winner Lee Wallard was so horribly burned a few days after he was crowned champion that he spent months in a hospital and had to undergo 37 operations. He never raced again.

Kelly Petillo, the 1935 winner, paid dues to the strange jinx by going to prison for years. Other winners, like Joe Dawson, Mauri Rose, Wilbur Shaw, Bill Vukovich and Bob Sweikert, all met violent deaths!

Tommy Milton, the Hall of Fame immortal who was the first man to win the classic twice, met a violent end. He was found shot to death.

There has never been another jinx like it in sports history — a jinx that has been hounding the winners of the "world series" of auto racing and dooming almost all of them.

The Unluckiest Ring Champion

One night early in June, 1923, Eugene Criqui became the world's featherweight champion. It was in many respects the most amazing ring victory of modern times.

When Eugene Criqui came from France to the United States to battle for the 126-pound title then held by Johnny Kilbane, who hadn't been defeated in 12 years (the longest fistic reign in history), he was already a man returned from the dead!

A veteran of the First World War, Criqui had been badly wounded during one historic battle in which about half-a-million soldiers were killed. Indeed, he had been given up for dead. Nonetheless, after four days of being lost amidst the casualties on that bloody battlefield, he was found with a glimmer of life miraculously still in him and rushed to a hospital, where doctors saved his life.

Eugene Criqui recovered from his wounds, but he came out of the hospital without a jaw. It had been shattered by a shell and replaced by a silver plate.

After the war, despite his physical handicap, Eugene Criqui returned to boxing. He was the only prizefighter with an artificial jaw.

That was the Frenchman who, on the night of June 2, 1923, climbed into the ring to face the great Johnny Kilbane for the world's featherweight championship. Game Eugene Criqui achieved an unforgettable ring victory when he knocked out his opponent in six rounds and became the new champ!

But the amazing pugilist with the artificial jaw had the briefest reign of any ring champ ever. His reign as featherweight champion lasted only 56 days!

Yes, only 56 days after his memorable June 2nd victory Eugene Criqui defended his title against the immortal Johnny Dundee, now in boxing's Hall of Fame. In a furious 15-rounder, the little Frenchman was dethroned by a referee's decision. Eugene Criqui never came back. Soon after the loss of his featherweight title, he quit the ring, and nothing was heard of him again.

Eugene Criqui holds a firm place in boxing memory. There never was a gamer man to step into a ring — and because his reign lasted no more than 56 days, he might be considered the unluckiest of all ring champs.

The Longest Prizefight

In 1893, when the legendary lightweight champion of the world, Jack McAuliffe, retired from the ring, even though he was still undefeated, two outstanding lightweights promptly laid claim to the vacated title. They were Andy Bowen and Jack Burke.

Hence, both of these boxers were matched to engage in a battle for the coveted crown on April 6, 1893, at the Olympic Club in New Orleans, Louisiana. The bout was to be fought with boxing gloves, in three-minute rounds — to a finish. The purse was twenty-five hundred dollars — winner take all.

At nine o'clock that evening the Bowen-Burke fight began before a frenzied crowd of boxing fans that jammed the arena to the rafters. From the opening round, it was a savage and brutal brawl, since both fighters were grimly determined to win as quickly as possible.

Round after tedious round, Andy Bowen and Jack Burke battled fiercely. After fifty rounds, neither fighter had gone down for a count, or weakened.

WHOO! THEY GOT TO CUT THESE THINGS DOWN TO A TOP OF A HUNNERT ROUNDS

Grimly and stubbornly, they fought on, each passing round filled with three minutes of furious action.

The ring battle dragged on far into the night. It went on to eighty, ninety, one hundred rounds! But neither fighter gave ground, as both remained on their feet, savagely pounding away at each other.

The grueling contest went on for an unbelievable total of seven hours and nineteen minutes. Finally, at the end of the 110th round, the two rugged lightweights were so battered and exhausted that both refused to come out of their corners for the 111th round.

Whereupon the referee of that incredible marathon boxing bout went to the center of the ring and announced his decision to the waiting crowd. The longest slugfest ever fought with boxing gloves was "no contest!"

Tragically, the two boxers who fought that 110-round battle for empty glory paid dearly for their endurance feat. Jack Burke never again fought in the ring. And when Andy Bowen returned to engage in a bout against the famous lightweight, George ("Kid") Lavigne, he not only lost the fight by a knockout in eighteen rounds, but also his life!

The Winning Streak That Stretched to Nowhere

In big-league baseball competition, the team that experienced the weirdest season of empty glory was the New York Giants of 1916, then piloted by none other than John J. McGraw, the most fabulous manager of all time. He was the first in history to win ten pennants, and to this day that feat hasn't been topped.

At the beginning of the 1916 season, the New York Giants got off to a drab start, losing ten of their first twelve games played at home. But driven hard by "Muggsy" McGraw, the Giants went on the road and ran up seventeen victories in a row. To this day, it has remained the longest winning streak by a major-league team playing away from its home ballpark.

As the season progressed, the Giants had their ups and downs. When September came, the final month of that campaign, the Giants were in fourth place in the National League race — thirteen games away from the top.

It was then that the hard-driven Giants produced

an unbelievable team effort in pursuit of the flag. It all began on September 7, when the Giants opened a final stand at home with a victory. They won again the next day. Then, on the afternoon of September 9, a durable hurler named Pel Perritt pitched a complete double-header for the Giants and won both games. His feat so inspired the pennant-hungry Giants that they continued to win day after day, game after game, playing against every team in the league. During that September of 1916, the incredible Giants achieved the all-time longest winning streak of modern major-league history — an unbelievable total of twenty-six victories in a row! No other big-league team has equaled that winning streak in a single season.

But that long winning streak was tarnished with bitter and heartbreaking disappointment for the heroes who accomplished the incomparable feat. When the New York Giants began their fantastic drive, they were in fourth place of their league standings. But after rolling up twenty-six consecutive victories in pursuit of the National League pennant, they **still** finished the 1916 season just where they had started — in fourth place of their league standings!

53

The Vanished Hockey Hero

Boyish-faced Bill Barilko was hardly 18 years old when he hit the big time as a defenseman for the Toronto Maple Leafs. Despite his youth, he was as rugged and phenomenal a player as could be found in the National Hockey League. His opponents all hurt when he hit them in the heat of competition. Once, he body-checked a rival with such force that he almost killed him. As the season passed, Bill Barilko established himself as the league's most punishing body-checker.

But tough as he was, Bill Barilko won everyone's respect, and all liked the carefree, happy-go-lucky bachelor for the "good guy" he was to have around. Big-league hockey became Barilko's life. Often he told his teammates: "The sun is really shining for me now!"

In 1951, when Bill Barilko was in his fifth season, he played like a demon in every game to help the Toronto Maple Leafs get into the Stanley Cup playoffs — and he played even harder in the final round of that "world series" against the formidable Montreal Canadiens.

In the third minute of a sudden-death overtime, in the fifth game of the 1951 Stanley Cup play-off final, with the Toronto Maple Leafs leading three games to one, it was Bill Barilko who swatted the puck over the head of the Canadiens' goalkeeper for the winning goal. With that, the Stanley Cup, symbol of the world's hockey championship, went to the Maple Leafs.

Bill Barilko was carried off the ice on the shoulders of his joyous teammates. Only after his supreme moment of glory had been achieved was it discovered that plucky Bill Barilko had played all through the final game with a broken nose.

When he departed for home with the praise and the well wishes of his teammates, he promised to return to play for them better than ever. But neither he nor they knew what fate had in store.

Shortly after his return home in Ontario, on the lower rim of the Canadian wilderness, Bill Barilko and a friend took off in a private plane for a weekend of fishing. When the famous hockey star failed to return, an alarm went out for the missing plane.

The Royal Canadian Air Force ordered 20 planes to fly over the wild bush country for any sign of the private plane's whereabouts. The search went on for days, and the Toronto Maple Leafs offered a reward of $10,000 to anyone finding the missing star, dead or alive. In all, the searching planes flew 1,345 hours, at a cost of $385,000, to find Bill Barilko, but it was all to no avail.

The disappearance was complete for nearly eleven years. But one day, in the bush country, hardly more than a hundred miles from Bill Barilko's home town, the wrecked plane was found. All that was left of Barilko was a skeleton for identification. It was a macabre end for a young man who, by the time he was only 23, had already won fame as a hockey great.

Danger for the Umpire

In 1899, Samuel White was umpiring a game between two professional teams in Lowndesborough, Alabama, when in a late inning a player began an argument over a close decision. Suddenly, the angry ballplayer went berserk and attacked the umpire, but the umpire knocked him down with a well-timed punch. Thereupon, the irate player grabbed a bat, swung it, and crushed the umpire's skull with it, killing him.

Shocking as that occurrence was for baseball's history book, a few years later, in another game played in Indiana, an umpire named Ora Jennings was also killed by an irate player. He, too, was struck on the head with a bat, following an argument over the umpire's decision.

Billy Evans, a fearless ump, was often threatened by angry ballplayers for "calling 'em as he saw 'em." Only one player ever stepped beyond the threatening stage with him and took action. Fabulous Ty Cobb, considered by many as the greatest ballplayer of all time, was the culprit. He got into an argument with Evans over a decision and he challenged the ump to meet him under the stands after the game. Billy Evans, who fancied himself something of a fist fighter, accepted.

While Evans fully expected his confrontation to be a scientific boxing match. Ty Cobb was no fighter by the rules. The moment Evans arrived under the stands, he grabbed the ump by the tie and almost choked him to death. Eventually, Billy Evans freed himself, and engaged Ty Cobb in a furious slugfest that lasted several minutes. But Ty Cobb, a tough man in a rough-and-ready brawl, punched and kicked Billy Evans to the floor and began banging his head on the concrete surface until he was dragged off the battered and almost unconscious umpire. He might have maimed him seriously if he had not been stopped.

Another time, there was an even more violent assault upon George Moriarty, who for 25 years was one of the toughest and most courageous umpires on the diamond.

One afternoon, in a game between the Chicago White Sox and the Cleveland Indians, Moriarty incurred the displeasure of the White Sox players, and they harassed and ridiculed him unmercifully. Moriarty ignored most of the savage taunts from the dugout, but promised the White Sox players that he would do something later about their foul insults.

As soon as the game was over, George Moriarty invaded the White Sox locker room and challenged anyone to repeat the name-calling to his face. No one player took up the challenge. Instead, about ten players ganged up on the courageous ump and physically attacked him. The most vehement rough-and-tumble brawl ever fought between players and umpire exploded then and there.

Finally, after almost 30 minutes of agitated fury, several White Sox players were spread out on the floor, unconscious — and the badly battered umpire had a broken arm.

Never again did any player dare "jockey" umpire George Moriarty with insults or pick a fight with him.

Don't Hurt Mother on Mother's Day

In May, 1939, when young Bob Feller was in his third season in the major leagues and establishing himself as one of baseball's most spectacular pitchers, he decided to give his mother a special treat. She had never seen him pitch in the major leagues, so, on the traditional Mother's Day holiday, Bob Feller brought his mother to Chicago from her farm in Iowa to watch him hurl a game for the Cleveland Indians against the Chicago White Sox.

His happy mother came to the Chicago ballpark, and sat in a box seat bedecked with flowers. It was indeed a rare treat to watch her famous son pitch in a big-league game for the first time. It was happiness beyond compare, inasmuch as it was she who had helped and encouraged him during his boyhood to aim for a baseball career.

When the game started, Bob Feller pitched brilliantly, as usual. In an early inning, however, a White Sox batter facing him swung desperately at one of his famed speedballs and just managed to foul it off. The ball sailed into the crowded stands, and ironically, although there were more than 40,000 people seated there, it plummeted toward Bob Feller's mother, struck her on the head, and knocked her unconscious!

Injured Ma Feller was rushed to a hospital, where a sad, shaken, and frightened Bob Feller kept vigil at her bedside until she was out of all danger. He was so distraught that he actually wanted to quit the game. In true tradition, however, his mother advised him not to blame himself at all, and encouraged him to "stay in there and pitch."

It was well that he did. Bob Feller went on to become one of the greatest pitchers in baseball, and then also entered the Hall of Fame as one of its honored immortals.

AVE ATQUE VALE, PAL

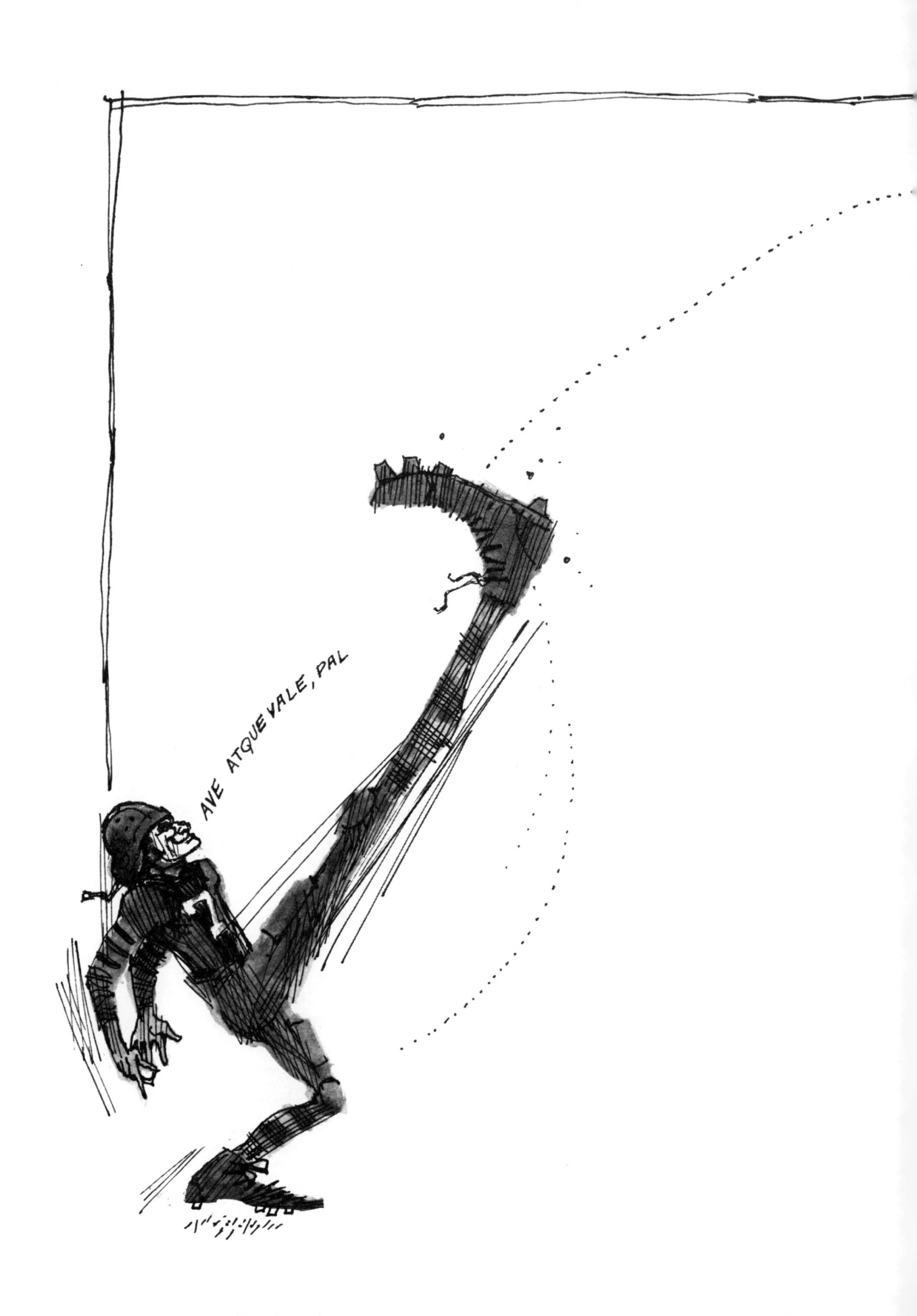

The Hero Who Disappeared

The strange and intriguing tale of Pat O'Dea, America's first authentic college football hero, goes back a long time. Born in Australia, where he achieved early athletic fame as a teen-age swimmer and sprinter, Pat O'Dea never saw a football game until he came to the United States to enroll as a student at the University of Wisconsin.

In 1896, freshman Pat O'Dea not only tried out for the Wisconsin football team and made it, but quickly became the most spectacular player of his time, so he remained for four consecutive seasons.

A rugged, speedy, and clever halfback who always played sixty minutes of every game, Pat O'Dea achieved supreme gridiron glory as a kicker. Nicknamed "The Kangaroo," he became the nonpareil punter and placement-kicker of all college football.

In his time, he punted top-rated opponents into submission and defeat with field goals from incredible distances. Sixty-yard field goals were the rule with him. He could kick them on muddy fields, against howling winds, or in blinding blizzards. Once, he was seen punting a football for a distance of 100 yards!

Pat O'Dea's precision kicking in intercollegiate gridiron play made him a legend in his lifetime, a national sports idol. He attracted hordes of admiring fans wherever he went, and was often besieged by them.

Even when his playing years were over, Pat O'Dea remained the most glamorous and most famous football hero in America! Legends still grew about him, and he was never free from legions of frenzied admirers.

The adulation showered upon him turned his private life into a shambles, so one day, Pat O'Dea simply vanished! For years, there were all sorts of wild rumors about his whereabouts, but eventually, most people came to assume that he was dead and buried in some unknown grave.

Then, one day, seventeen years after his mysterious disappearance, football's long-lost immortal was found very much alive. Pat O'Dea was living and working in peaceful obscurity in a small town under the name of Charles Mitchell. His neighbors knew nothing of his past.

When his true identity was revealed, Pat O'Dea confessed that he had vanished to escape the burden of his awesome football fame.

Thus ended the most puzzling disappearance in football history!

Happy Jack's Wild Pitch

His name was John Dwight Chesbro, but during his eleven years in the major leagues he was known as "Happy Jack," because this handsome, rough-and-tough, but good-natured right-handed pitcher was one of the happiest players around. One of the outstanding pitchers of his time, winner of two hundred major-league games, he has an honored place in baseball's Hall of Fame.

In 1904, when "Happy Jack" Chesbro was the star

pitcher for the New York Yankees, then known as the Highlanders, he achieved a feat never equaled by any other hurler. In that season, he won an astonishing total of forty-one games.

But strangely, his most glorious season ended with a humiliation and a disaster that was to haunt him for the rest of his life.

On the final day of that 1904 season, "Happy Jack" Chesbro went to the mound in an effort to win his forty-second game of that year and clinch the American League pennant for his team. In the ninth inning, with the bases full of opposition runners, on the final play, mighty Chesbro threw a wild pitch that brought in the winning run. He not only lost the game, but also the pennant.

For the rest of his life, "Happy Jack" Chesbro was unfairly remembered as the man who wild-pitched his team out of the pennant race in the final game of his most glorious winning year.

The Endurable Baseball Player

On the afternoon of May 2, 1939, shortly before the world championship New York Yankees were about to take the field in a game against the Detroit Tigers, their captain, Lou Gehrig, approached Joe McCarthy, the Yankee manager.

"I guess you'd better put someone else on first base today," he announced. "I'm no help to your ball club."

The Yankee pilot's words belied his emotions. He shrugged his shoulders and simply replied, "Whatever you say, Lou!"

Moments before the start of that game, Lou Gehrig had walked up to the chief umpire and handed him the team's batting order. The ump casually glanced at it, but then his eyes widened and his mouth popped open with surprise, for he saw the name of Babe Dahlgren written on it to play first base for the Yankees.

"What's up, Lou?" asked the astonished umpire. "Aren't you playing first, as usual?" But he quickly stopped asking questions, and turned away with a lump in his throat. The famous first baseman, Lou Gehrig, sadly shook his head. There were tears in his eyes.

The startling news that Gehrig wasn't going to play for the Yankees struck the fans in the ballpark like a thunderbolt. The news spread quickly, and before the game was over, the whole baseball world knew that the famed "Iron Horse" of the diamond had snapped an incredible consecutive playing streak. But he had set an endurance record that will never be equaled!

It had taken him fifteen consecutive seasons and untold physical hardships to create that record. Lou Gehrig had played first base for the Yankees in 2,130 consecutive major-league games!

To keep the playing streak alive, game after game and season after season, the "Iron Horse" had played despite beatings, cracked ribs, chipped bones, broken fingers, broken toes, muscle tears, wrenched shoulders, pulled ligaments, and lumbago attacks. The amazing

Lou Gehrig refused to seize upon a single accident as an excuse to miss a contest.

And what imperishable glory Lou Gehrig also achieved during that playing streak! He not only became one of the finest fielding first basemen of all time, but also one of the greatest hitters. There were seasons when he hit .351, .354, .363, .373, .374, and .379 — to compile an astounding lifetime batting average of .340! He became the first modern player to hit four home runs in a row in one nine-inning game. Only he slugged as many as twenty-three "grand slam" homers, hit a total of 494 home runs in all, and helped the Yankees win seven pennants!

After taking himself out of the Yankee line-up that day, Lou Gehrig never again played for the Yankees. But, in tribute to their great captain, the team went on to win its fourth straight pennant and fourth consecutive World Series championship that season.

Hardly two years later, at age 38, he was dead, the tragic victim of a mysterious disease.

So ended the saga of Lou Gehrig, once the most endurable player.

Sweet Retribution

In the 1940 football season, the Chicago Bears were as formidable a team as ever played. They were called "The Monsters of the Midway." All teams fell before them — except one. In an early game during that season, the Bears became a bit careless and lost a squeaker to the Washington Redskins — then spearheaded by the immortal Sammy Baugh, perhaps the greatest quarterback of all time — by a score of 7 to 3.

At the conclusion of that season, a malicious fate brought about a curious playoff finish. The Chicago Bears and the Washington Redskins, by virtue of their triumphs, were scheduled to meet to decide the National Football League championship.

Before the big game took place, however, the

owner, coach and some of the players of the Washington Redskins club committed an unpardonable boner. They publicly mocked the Chicago Bears, and even ridiculed their awesome reputation.

So, on a balmy Sunday afternoon, December 8, 1940, "The Monsters of the Midway" came to the nation's capital to battle the Washington Redskins in jampacked Griffith Stadium for the pro football championship of the world.

The game was hardly forty seconds old when the angry Bears stunned 50,000 deriding Washington fans by scoring their first touchdown. Before the bewildered Redskins knew what had happened, the Bears scored second and third touchdowns — and turned the event into a lopsided farce.

In the fury of their assault on the Washington Redskins, the "Monsters of the Midway" rolled up 372 yards rushing, while holding their opponents to a mere three yards. The Chicago Bears continued to pile up the score, with almost every player contributing to the historic rout. They galloped to eleven touchdowns, using ten different players to score them, and six different men kicked the conversions after touchdowns.

The final score of the game was an unbelievable 73-0. It was the highest score ever recorded in a championship football game; and even more, it was the highest score ever achieved by a pro football team in a single competition!

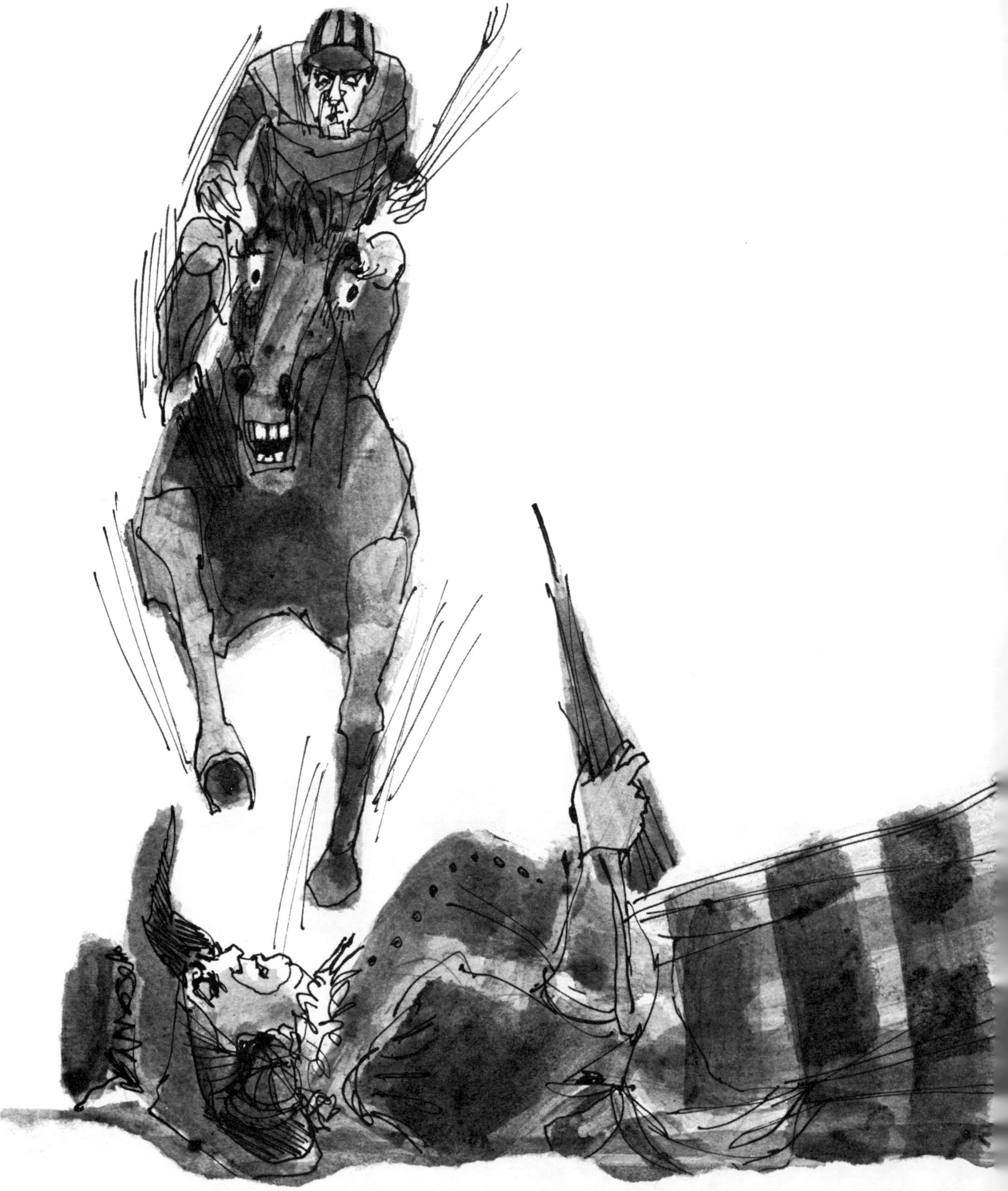

A Race Horse That Changed History

A race horse galloping toward a victory in a famed turf classic once trampled a woman to death under its hoofs — and thereupon precipitated a significant change in the government of a nation.

In 1913, England was in a turmoil over the controversial question of women's suffrage. Militant suffragettes throughout the country demanded that the women of England be granted the right to vote in national elections, as was the privilege of all male British citizens. But a reluctant Parliament was in no hurry to resolve the stormy political issue.

Came a day in June of 1913 and time for the running of England's annual premier horse race, the Epsom Derby. More than 300,000 Britishers from all walks of life came to witness the important turf event. Of particular interest to most spectators was a race horse named Anmer, an overwhelming favorite to win.

It was owned by no less a notable than the King of England, George V.

As Anmer came thundering down the homestretch, well in the lead, and seemingly a sure winner of the race, a suffragette, Emily Davidson, ran onto the race track. Waving a banner and shouting, "Long live women's suffrage!" she deliberately threw herself into the path of the royal race horse. Before any of the horrified spectators could fully realize what was happening, she was trampled and killed.

Thousands of women from all over England came to mourn at the funeral of suffragette Emily Davidson. Her bizarre and ultimate act during the Epsom Derby stirred such a stormy pitch that a harassed Parliament was forced to act quickly and pass a law without further delay granting the women of England the right to vote.

Anmer the race horse lost the 1913 Epsom Derby, and a suffragette lost her life, but a giant step was gained for the political rights of England's women.

The Pitching Feat Didn't Count

Harvey Haddix, at age 33, once achieved the most incredible feat of perfect pitching ever witnessed in a major-league baseball game — but it didn't count for his glory as a winning hurler.

On May 26, 1959, this southpaw pitching veteran went to the mound to pitch for the Pittsburgh Pirates against the league-leading Milwaukee Braves, then featuring in their lineup several of the most imposing hitters in the National League.

On that day, Harvey Haddix was nursing a cold. He thought he would be lucky if he could get through nine innings without being blasted out of the box.

At the end of nine innings of play, however, Harvey was still on the mound for the Pirates, and he had achieved a rare pitching miracle. The small-sized southpaw had faced twenty-seven enemy batters, and he had mowed down all twenty-seven in a row without a hit, a walk, or a run. It was a perfect nine-inning no-hitter.

But the game wasn't over for Harvey. His teammates had failed to produce even a single run for him to complete the game. So the game went into extra innings, and stout-hearted Harvey Haddix continued to keep the miracle going for the amazement of the awed spectators in the stands.

He didn't yield a hit nor a walk to any of the batters who faced him in the tenth inning, the eleventh, or the twelfth. Thirty-six batsmen in a row mowed down! It was an unequalled feat of perfect no-hit pitching in one game. But still the game wasn't over for Harvey Haddix, because his teammates had failed to score.

Eventually, disaster exploded the pitching miracle into ashes. In the thirteenth inning, an error and a dubious hit lost the game for Harvey and the Pirates by a score of 1 to 0.

Thus it happened that Harvey Haddix became the only major-league pitcher to hurl as many as twelve perfect no-hit no-run innings in one game — but although he had achieved the longest one-game perfect hurling feat, it didn't count!

A Ballplayer's Nightmare

Eddie Waitkus goes back to the 1940's. He was as good a first baseman as could be found in baseball. But he was more than an outstanding big-league star. He was a handsome man, and one of the most popular players of his time. Wherever he played, a horde of admirers were on his trail, many of them female fans.

On the afternoon of June 15, 1940, the Philadelphia Phillies played a scheduled game in Chicago against the Cubs, and Waitkus, at first base for the Phillies, was the star of that game. It was a most happy day for him, until he returned to his hotel. There the desk clerk handed him a message requesting him to come to a particular room in regard to a most important matter. Puzzled and curious, Eddie Waitkus went there to find out what it was all about.

When he entered the room to which he had been summoned, he faced a nineteen-year-old girl who was a total stranger to him. She confronted him with a gun in her hand, pointed directly at him.

She told him that she was a baseball fan, and that he was her hero. Then she berated him for ignoring all the notes she had sent expressing her admiration and love. Before Eddie Waitkus could calm down the girl, she shot him. The famous ballplayer fell to the floor with a bullet in his chest.

Thirty-year-old Eddie Waitkus, near death, was rushed to a hospital. The disturbed girl who had attempted to murder him was taken away by the police.

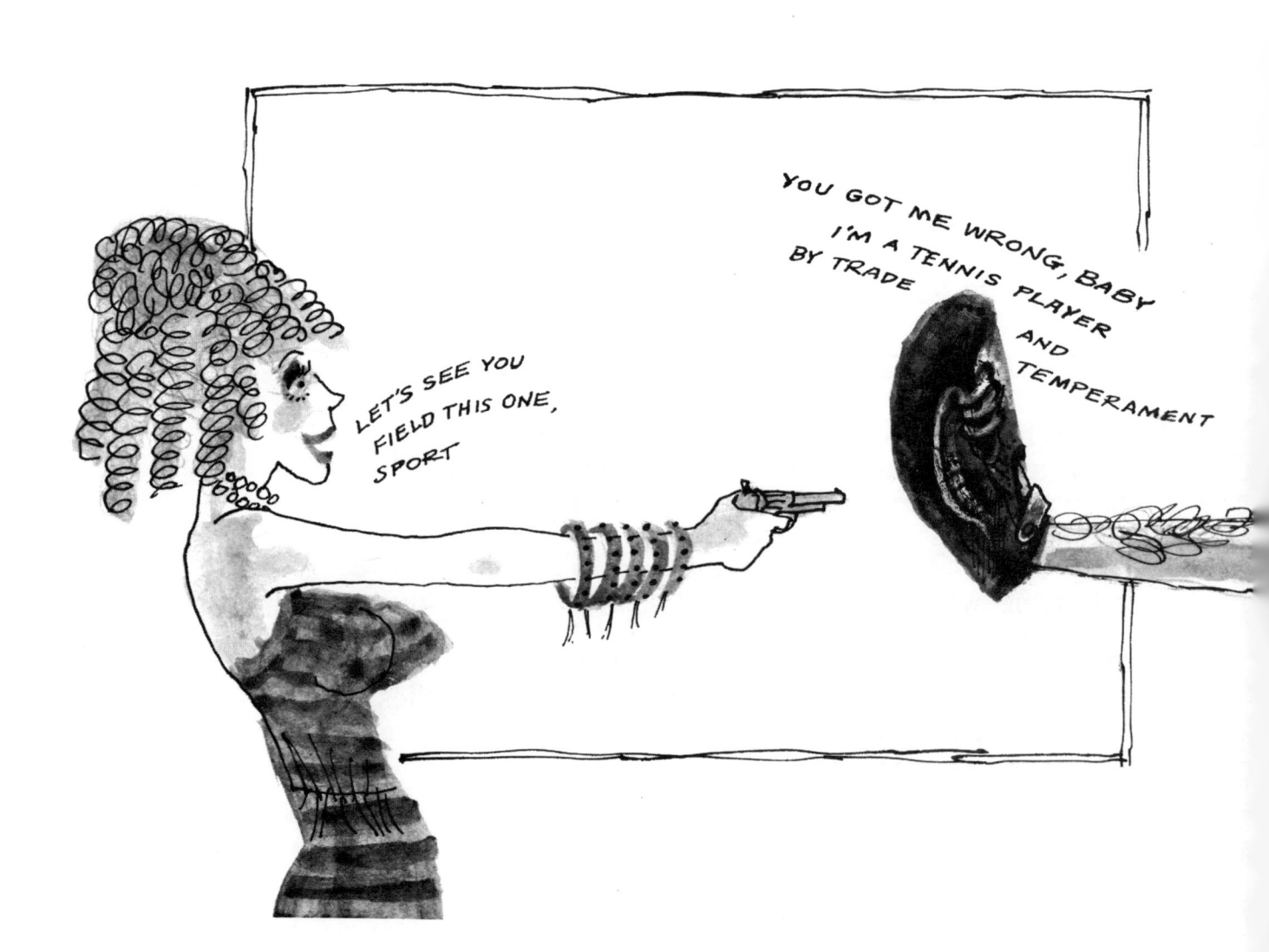

Eddie Waitkus underwent four surgical operations. It was a miracle that the doctors saved his life. It was another miracle that he recovered sufficiently to return the following season to resume playing first base for the Philadelphia Phillies.

Surprisingly, there was a happy ending to Eddie Waitkus' brush with death. He played so brilliantly in his miraculous comeback that he sparked the Philadelphia Phillies to win the National League pennant in 1950 — their first flag triumph in thirty-five years.

The Murdered Race Horse

In May of every year, at Pimlico race track in Maryland, the world's fastest three-year-old thoroughbreds run for turf glory in the Preakness, America's oldest horse race. It has been the only race in the world to honor and keep green the memory of a murdered horse.

It was back in the 19th century, that a horse named Preakness came into the turf world. Preakness was ugly in looks, ungainly in form, and ponderous in size (he stood seventeen hands high). As a thoroughbred destined for racing fame, Preakness was mocked and ridiculed as a cart horse.

In 1870, when the Maryland Jockey Club staged the first race at newly built Pimlico race track for the outstanding three-year-old thoroughbreds in America, Preakness romped home an easy winner.

From that glorious victory, ugly-duckling Preakness went on to become America's winningest, best-loved, and most famous race horse — a national turf idol.

In 1876, on a visit to the United States, a noted British sportsman, the Duke of Hamilton, saw Preakness win a race. He became so fascinated with the famous race horse that he paid a fortune to buy Preakness from its owner. Preakness was shipped off to England to grace the racing stables owned by the Duke of Hamilton.

Soon after his purchase of Preakness, the Duke of Hamilton visited his racing stable. When he tried to pet Preakness, the horse somehow became so disturbed that it almost killed its owner. Whereupon, the Duke became so enraged that he promptly fetched a gun and fired two bullets into the head of that famous race horse, killing it instantly.

When the senseless killing of Preakness by his irate owner became public knowledge, it caused widespread shock. It stirred up such a storm of public indignation throughout England that prompt reforms and laws were initiated governing the humane treatment of horses. It actually became a crime for any horse owner to mistreat his animal, or to exercise cruelty and violence upon it.

And in the United States an unusual and lasting honor was bestowed upon Preakness to keep its memory alive. The Maryland Jockey Club established an annual turf race at Pimlico race track for the world's fastest and greatest three-year-old thoroughbreds — to be known always as The Preakness.

To this day, the annual Preakness turf classic is the event held to honor the memory of a legendary race horse!

A Baseball Game Without End

The longest game (by innings) in baseball history was played between the old Boston Braves and the former Brooklyn Dodgers at Braves Field, Boston, on May 1, 1920. That contest also produced the most tireless "iron-man" pitching duel ever seen. Despite all that, it went down in the books as "no contest!"

There was a faint drizzle in the air on that cold, damp, Saturday afternoon when umpire Barry McCormick called "Play ball!" A slim gathering of only 4,000 fans huddled in the stands.

Joe Oeschger, a fast-ball journeyman pitcher, was on the mound for the Braves, and curve-ball specialist Leon Cadore hurled for the Dodgers. Neither pitcher was considered especially outstanding. Neither of the two had an inkling that fate had brought them together to exhibit the most unbelievable marathon performance ever seen on the diamond.

Nothing important happened until the first half of the fifth inning, when the Dodgers scored a run. Then, in the last half of the sixth inning, the Braves also scored a run, and the game was deadlocked 1-1.

Thereafter, the two rival pitchers settled down to scoreless hurling, and the scoreboard registered zeros inning after inning. The game was still tied at the end of nine innings of play, so it went into extra innings, with each of the two starting pitchers remaining on the mound.

Each man continued to pitch for nine more innings, and neither Joe Oeschger or Leon Cadore tired or would quit to give way for a relief hurler. Thus, they went into the nineteenth and twentieth innings — and **still** the score remained tied at one run for each team!

The two teams completed the twenty-first, twenty-second, twenty-third, and twenty-fourth innings, and still Joe Oeschger and Leon Cadore were in there pitching. Each breezed through the twenty-fifth and twenty-sixth innings. Cadore had pitched now twenty successive scoreless innings for his team; and Oeschger had pitched twenty-one shutout frames in a row for his team. It was a record for consecutive scoreless pitching by two opposing hurlers in one major-league game.

But this extraordinary baseball game became a wasted effort for all the players of both teams, and especially for the two stalwart pitchers who had presided on the mound, because there was no winner and no loser. At the conclusion of the twenty-sixth inning, umpire Barry McCormick finally halted the game "on account of darkness." He was as exhausted as the players.

Thus came to a meaningless end the longest major-league baseball game ever played.

The Unluckiest World Series Pitcher

Ever since the inception of the World Series, in 1903, baseball pitchers have nursed dreams and hopes of achieving imperishable hurling glory in that competition. Throughout the years, many have written their names into the history of the October classic with unforgettable pitching feats.

Conversely, a host of major-league pitchers have also written their names into World Series history as unforgettable losers, the unluckiest being Charlie Root. No other hurler was ever victimized by World Series misfortune as often as Charlie Root, who pitched for the Chicago Cubs for 16 years, hurled them to four pennants, and wound up winning more than 200 major-league games. But it was Charlie Root's destiny to become a "World Series sucker" more times than any other pitcher performing in the championship classic.

Charlie Root appeared as a pitcher for the first time in a World Series in 1929. He was given the honor of hurling the opening game, and he was an overwhelming favorite to win it against the former Philadelphia Athletics. His pitching opponent was a surprise and unexpected starter — the aged, washed-up hurler, Howard Ehmke, who throughout the regular season had pitched less than 50 innings. Capable Charlie Root against old and faded Howard Ehmke was considered a ludicrous mismatch.

But it was Charlie Root who wound up as the outstanding "sucker" of the World Series opener. Ehmke suddenly regained the hurling magic of his youth, pitched a masterpiece, and struck out a record 13 batters to win in style.

The next misfortune for unlucky Charlie came in the fourth game of that 1929 World Series. At the start of the 7th inning, breezing along to an easy victory by a score of 8 to 0, he had allowed only two measly hits to the opposition. But then he happened to throw a fast ball to Al Simmons, the Athletics' most dangerous slugger — and Simmons connected for a home run. That blow triggered the most unbelievable batting rally in World Series history. Before the inning was over, the Athletics scored a record ten runs, and won the game! Once again, Charlie Root emerged from a World Series battle tarnished with the onus of "pitching sucker."

Charlie Root didn't show up in World Series play again until three years later, when he pitched the third game of the 1932 World Series against the New York Yankees, led by the legendary Babe Ruth, the home-run slugger! The immortal "Bambino" was then pot-bellied and thirty-seven years old, playing in his tenth and final World Series.

Again, Charlie Root became the fall guy of an unforgettable World Series drama. When the mighty Babe came to bat in a late inning, with the score tied, the hostile Chicago fans poured merciless heckling upon him. (He had already hit one home run in that game.) Wildly, they screamed for pitcher Charlie Root to strike out "the bum." And Charlie Root poured across home plate two quick strikes on Babe Ruth.

Then Babe Ruth did something never before seen in a World Series, and likely never to be seen again. Deliberately, he pointed to a far-off spot in the bleacher stands, indicating where he was going to drive his next home run. It stirred the crowd into a wild frenzy of jeering. But when Charlie Root hurled his next pitch, Babe Ruth tagged it for a home run, sending it to the very spot he had pointed to. It was the most dramatic, unforgettable home run ever hit. It won the game, and once again Charlie Root emerged as a World Series loser.

Three years later, Charlie Root again pitched a game in a World Series, and again he lost. And then, three years after that, he pitched in the 1938 October classic, and again he lost. Six times he pitched in World Series games over a full decade, and each time the result was disastrous. No wonder he was labeled the unluckiest of all pitchers in World Series history!

The Baseball Holdout With a Secret

Before the start of every baseball season, a number of players have always engaged in a "holdout" battle with their respective club owners on the matter of salary. Many of them have staged unforgettable battles, ultimately winning or losing bitter disputes over salary contracts. The strangest holdout was Urban Shocker, who truly created a shocker of a holdout tale for the record.

In his time, Urban Shocker was an outstanding pitcher, good enough to win two hundred games during his stay in the big leagues.

In 1928, before the start of the regular baseball season, when Urban Shocker was thirty-six years old and still starring for the then-fabulous pennant-winning New York Yankees, he refused to sign a new contract unless he was given a modest two-thousand dollar raise in his annual salary. He felt entitled to such a boost, because the season before he had been an 18-game winner. When the club owner snubbed Shocker's demands, the aging hurler became a holdout. Proud and stubborn, he remained adamant all through the spring training season, and even after the regular campaign officially began.

Finally, the multi-millionaire New York club owner was shamed into a surrender, and Urban Shocker was given the salary raise he had demanded.

But after gaining his memorable holdout victory, Urban Shocker hardly pitched during tht 1928 season. He hurled only one game for the Yankees, and lost it.

Winning the holdout battle was Urban Shocker's greatest triumph of that baseball season, because all through his long and grim siege he hid a bitter secret, not not only from his club owner but from all his teammates. He was a dying man — the victim of an incurable disease that was snuffing out his life. Before the season ended, pitcher Urban Shocker was gone from this world.

The $100,000 Muff

Fred Snodgrass was a major-league ballplayer, and a most unusual one, but stangely, the baseball story for which he is remembered is one that he would have liked to forget. It haunted him almost to the last day of his long life.

It was early in the century when Fred Snodgrass came out of Ventura, California, to make his mark. He was 21 then, and the New York Giants, piloted by John McGraw, paid him a salary of $150 a month. But money didn't matter much to Fred Snodgrass, because he was on his way to glory with a fabulous team.

An aggressive player and a fair hitter, Fred Snodgrass became an outstanding center fielder in the major leagues. He was fleet-footed and a sure-handed fly hawk in the outfield, often making spectacular catches to save ball games for his team.

His valuable efforts more than satisfied John McGraw, the toughest manager there ever was. Fred Snodgrass, with glove, bat, and fighting spirit, helped win three pennants for the Giants during his eight seasons with them.

In the 1912 World Series, Fred Snodgrass was the most talked-about ballplayer. Great outfielder though he was, he committed one error that became the costliest one in World Series annals.

In that World Series, the Giants played the Boston Red Sox for the baseball championship, and it went down to the final game, with three victories for each team. The deciding game went into the tenth inning. The Giants scored a run and needed only three more

SO EASY WHEN YOU GOT
A TON OF TALENT...
WHICH YOU GOT
TO ADMIT!

OOPS!?

PLOP!

outs to win the Series by a score of 2 to 1. It was almost a sure thing, since Hall-of-Famer Christy Mathewson was on the mound for the Giants.

But then something unthinkable happened that never happened to Fred Snodgrass before. In the last half of the tenth inning, pinch hitter ClydeEngle came up to bat for the Red Sox. He lofted an easy fly ball to center field, and Fred Snodgrass parked under it for an easy catch and a sure out. But, to his abject consternation, the ball dribbled through his fingers — for an error! Engle reached second base. The next batter walked, and then up to bat came Tris Speaker, who belted a long single which not only drove in the tying run, but also the winning run!

The error Fred Snodgrass made lost the World Series for the Giants and became known as the "$100,000 Muff." That was the difference between the winners' and the losers' share of the Series purse.

Fred Snodgrass's monumental error was to haunt him mercilessly. In 1916, his tenth season in the majors, even though he was starring for the Boston Braves, fans still taunted him with imitations of his muff of the fly ball that had lost the 1912 World Series. Finally, one day, during a big game, Fred Snodgrass reached the end of his patience. He walked up to the stands, faced his tormentors, and deliberately thumbed his nose at all the spectators. One of them was the Mayor of Boston. His ungentlemanly gesture created a furor!

That day, Fred Snodgrass quit as a major-league player forever! He was not yet 30 years old when it happened.

The Jockey Who Came Back from the Dead

One afternoon in 1936, a stunned crowd of more than 30,000 spectators at Bay Meadows race track in

California saw it happen. Ralph Neves was thrown from a race horse and carried off the track. They then heard the tragic official announcement, "We regret to inform you that, as a result of the accident in the last race, jockey Neves is dead! Please say a silent prayer for him."

Pronouncing jockey Ralph Neves dead was not the end of his story as a rider of race horses, however. Out of sight of the thousands of spectators a strange miracle came to pass.

When the jockey was duly examined by a doctor, no spark of life could be found in his battered body. His respiration had ceased, and he had no pulse or heartbeat.

"There's nothing more that can be done for him — he's dead!" declared the doctor.

So, an ambulance took the "dead jockey" to a mortuary. But some minutes after the body of Ralph Neves was placed on a cold slab with an identifying tag around his neck, a doctor friend of his arrived, and purely on a hunch, he injected a shot of adrenalin into the dead jockey's heart.

To everyone's shocked surprise, Ralph Neves suddenly came back from the dead. He opened his eyes and growled, "Where am I? What's going on here?"

From that day on, little Ralph Neves, known as the "Portuguese Pepperpot," became famous as the jockey they couldn't bury. And, as the years went by, he lived up to that reputation to the hilt. Again and again he survived tragic spills to amaze doctors and defy the odds against him. Twice his back was broken. Once his skull was cracked, and another time, half his body was paralyzed. On six different occasions, doctors gloomily told him that he would never again ride a race horse; and three times, after bad spills, his injuries seemed so serious that he was given last rites.

But jockey Ralph Neves always came back to ride race horses to fame and fortune. Hung together with stitches, metal braces, tape, and courage, jockey Ralph Neves — who was once pronounced dead — booted home 3,771 winners over the years, and won more than fifteen million dollars in turf purses!

The Wrong Derby Winner

For a jockey there is no greater triumph than riding a three-year-old thoroughbred to a victory in the Kentucky Derby, America's oldest and most exalted horse race. Almost all Derby-winner jockeys are now in turf's Hall of Fame as immortals of the horse racing sport.

But it so happened that a jockey once won a Kentucky Derby, and it was the biggest blunder of his life. The victory cost the owner of the winning horse a quarter-of-a-million dollars. And for winning the famed Run for the Roses gallop, the unfortunate jockey was not only beaten within an inch of his life, but he also became a turf outcast.

In 1921, Colonel Matt Winn Bradley, the owner of more Kentucky Derby winners than any other, owned a fine three-year-old thoroughbred named Black Servant. Naturally, it was entered in the Kentucky Derby, to enrich its fame as the fastest thoroughbred in the turf world. Black Servant was an all-out favorite to win the classic Run for the Roses, and so confident was its owner that he wagered a cool quarter-of-a-million dollars on Black Servant to win. The grooms and stable hands working for Colonel Bradley were of similar mind and wagered their own money as well.

To make sure that his favorite race horse would run its fastest and best race, shrewd owner Bradley entered another one of his fleet-footed thoroughbreds to run in that 1921 Kentucky Derby. Its name was Behave Yourself. Jockey Charlie Thompson was hired to ride it.

Before the race started, Charlie Thompson was given strict instructions by Colonel Bradley as to how to ride his horse. He was ordered to come out fast, grab the lead, and set an early fast pace for the favorite, Black Servant. He was to keep up the pressure until the homestretch, when Black Servant would take over the lead and romp across the finish line.

What jockey Charlie Thompson wasn't told at the time was that Colonel Bradley had placed the $250,000 bet on Black Servant to win.

When the race started, jockey Thompson followed his orders implicitly. He made an amazing ride on Behave Yourself, pacing Black Servant and holding the lead coming into the homestretch. It must have been then that Thompson suddenly coveted the glory of booting home a Derby winner. He disregarded all orders and refused to surrender the lead to Black Servant, galloping behind him almost neck and neck. As a result, in a thundering finish, Behave Yourself nosed out Black Servant to win the 1921 Kentucky Derby.

Even though Colonel Bradley had another Derby winner to his credit, he was furiously angry with jockey Charlie Thompson. The $250,000 wager placed on Black Servant, which had finished in second place, was lost. Triumphant jockey Thompson was promptly fired, and was bluntly informed that, for disobeying orders, Colonel Bradley would see to it that no other horse owner in Kentucky ever hired him again.

Moreover, when Charlie Thompson returned to his dressing room after his hollow triumph, another calamity awaited him. The grooms and stable hands who had wagered and lost their money ganged up on the unfortunate jockey and beat him mercilessly.

It was the most penalizing reward a jockey ever received for winning a Kentucky Derby.

The First Man to Swim the English Channel

On August 25, 1875, an Englishman, Captain Matthew Webb, became the first man to swim across the English Channel. He conquered the treacherous twenty-one-mile strip of water from England to France in twenty-one hours and forty-five minutes. Thirty-six years were to pass before another sturdy swimmer accomplished the Channel crossing, and to this day, hardly more than a hundred daring long-distance swimmers from all over the world have achieved this distinction.

Captain Matthew Webb's aquatic accomplishment was hailed as the epic feat of the century, and he became famous overnight. Everyone everywhere wanted to see that amazing Englishman. Webb quickly made a fortune appearing before awed audiences as the world's most daring long-distance swimmer.

Eventually, he came to the United States and was greeted warmly and enthusiastically everywhere. While on tour, the celebrity was challenged to a long-distance race by a swimmer known as Captain Paul Boynton, who had also performed some daring aquatic exploits. The two captains agreed to engage in a 25-mile race, starting from the beach in Newport, for a prize of one thousand dollars, plus a side bet of five thousand dollars — winner take all. The scheduled event stirred up interest and excitement on both sides of the Atlantic, and fortunes were wagered on the outcome.

When the time came for the start of the race, Captain Webb showed up wearing trunks, but Captain Boynton presented an odd appearance — he wore a non-sinkable pneumatic rubber swimming suit. The proud Englishman was so confident that he could outswim any human in a marathon that he consented to go through with the 25-mile race, even though the sly American was dressed in his rubber suit.

On a blowy September morning on the beach at Newport, the two rivals stepped gingerly into the cold water at a sign from the referee, and their swimming race began.

After only about ten miles in a heavy swell, Captain Matthew Webb was suddenly seized with cramps for the first time in his career, and he had to be pulled out of the water to be saved from drowning. But Captain Paul Boynton continued swimming until he finished the race, and collected the prize and the fame that went to the winner of that international contest.

Failure to complete the swimming race, and losing it, was a great humiliation for Matthew Webb. Because of his unexpected defeat, he came to believe that he had become the laughingstock of an amused American public. He thereupon attempted an impossible "first" in swimming history. He set out to conquer the roaring waters of Niagara Falls.

In his daring but heedless effort to swim the Niagara rapids, heroic Captain Matthew Webb, first swimmer to conquer the English Channel, came to a strange and ironic end. He drowned.

Never Give Up!

The longest fistic ring battle with boxing gloves fought between two heavyweights took place on April 17, 1909, in Paris, France. Curiously, it was a match between two once-famous American heavyweights, Joe Jeannette and Sam McVey, who were bosom pals outside the prize ring.

That unbelievable prizefight came about when those two good friends found themselves in gay Paris — broke. So, the two top-ranking heavyweights agreed to go 50 rounds for a $5,000 purse, to be equally divided.

It was not only the longest heavyweight bout ever fought with boxing gloves, but also the strangest ever fought between two famous heavyweights. For even though Joe Jeannette and Sam McVey were buddies, their friendship was forgotten as both fought furiously from the opening bell. They slugged each other from ring post to ring post. McVey knocked down Jeannette in every round, but Jeannette kept getting up after each knockdown, growling: "Come on, Sam! Let's do some real fighting!"

By the 40th round, Sam McVey had knocked down Joe Jeannette 39 times! By the end of the 49th round, Sam McVey was so tired, and so disgusted with his opponent's stubbornness, that he quit. He refused to come out for the 50th and final round of the bout. So, Joe Jeannette, who had been knocked down a total of 49 times, was declared to be the winner.

No prizefighter in history ever won a more incredible ring victory.

A Gallop to Ignominy

Never has a football season passed into history without contributing its quota of gridiron mistakes. But only a few were so startling that they became unforgettable. Perhaps the biggest boner of all was Roy

Riegels' extraordinary wrong-way run to gridiron ignominy.

In his time, Roy Riegels was an outstanding player. He was the center for a powerful University of California football team, and he was not only good enough to be its captain, but also to gain national distinction as an All-America hero. But a single mistake branded him forever as a tarnished hero for gridiron's supreme blunder.

On New Year's Day of 1929, more than 100,000 spectators were at the Rose Bowl game — the "daddy" of all annual Bowl classics — to witness a gridiron battle between two college titans, the University of California and mighty Georgia Tech, for the intercollegiate football championship.

Shortly after the start of the second quarter, with both teams deadlocked in a scoreless tie, a malicious fate chose Ray Riegels to embark on a strange gallop for touchdown glory. Following a fierce scrimmage, center Roy Riegels suddenly found himself in possession of a fumbled loose football. Under the rules then in effect, a player defending was eligible to run with an offensive fumble of the ball.

So, with the ball in his hands, an alert and happy Roy Riegels lit out on a run to the Georgia Tech goal. But after running for only a few yards, he lost his sense of direction as he attempted to dodge some enemy tacklers, and he now began to run toward his own goal line, more than 65 yards away.

Only one of his teammates, fleet-footed quarterback Benny Lom, quickly sensed the irrationality of Roy Riegels' course, and set out in pursuit of his team's confused captain, shouting at him to turn around. It was to no avail — the roar of the mob drowned out all other sounds for scampering Roy Riegels. Finally, Benny Lom caught up with him, and with a desperate lunge tackled him and fiercely brought him down to earth — less than a foot from California's own goal line.

When the dazed Roy Riegels realized the blunder he had committed, he burst into tears. Moments later, when the stunned California football team went into a punt formation behind its own goal line in an attempt to remedy Roy Riegels' long wrong-way run, the kick was blocked by a Georgia Tech player, and it resulted in a two-point safety score for Georgia Tech. It was the difference between a victory and a defeat. The memorable game ended with Georgia Tech the winner by a score of 8 to 7.

Overnight, heartbroken Roy Riegels became the most talked-about and most ridiculed football player. Newspaper headlines spread the amusing story of his wrong-way run far and wide. "Wrong-way Riegels" actually became a household word. Thereafter, anyone who committed a glaring mistake or inept blunder was promptly dubbed a "Wrong-way Riegels."

He was flooded with thousands of letters of sympathy or derision, written to him by people from all over the world. A host of girls proposed marriage with him. Hollywood offered to star him as a wrong-way hero of the screen. He was tempted with all sorts of lucrative commercial offers to capitalize on the notoriety of his wrong-way run in the Rose Bowl. But Roy Riegels rejected all offers and went into hiding to escape from unwanted fame.

Even after his college days were over, for years thereafter, wherever he went, and whatever he did, he was remembered as the football player who once ran the wrong way to lose a Rose Bowl game.

Roy Riegels' wrong-way gallop took less than fifteen seconds, but that was long enough for him to carve his name and "fame" into football history.

A Broken Leg For a Football Star

On November 9, 1912, a football team from the legendary Carlisle College for Indians, led by the immortal Jim Thorpe, played against a powerful team from West Point. The Indians from Carlisle trounced the cadets from the Military Academy of West Point by a score of 27 to 6.

That game became unique in sports history, because a husky Army player ambitiously tried to stop Jim Thorpe from scoring a touchdown, and was bowled over by the mighty Indian so violently that he wound up with a broken leg, never to play football again.

But that unfortunate West Point football player nevertheless acquired distinction as a most unusual gridiron warrior. He was the first college varsity football player to become the leader of a nation.

That West Point football player, whose career was suddenly cut short by Jim Thorpe, greatest football player of all time, became the 34th President of the United States — Dwight David ("Ike") Eisenhower.

HE AIN'T GEN. CUSTER, BUT HE'LL HAVE TO DO....

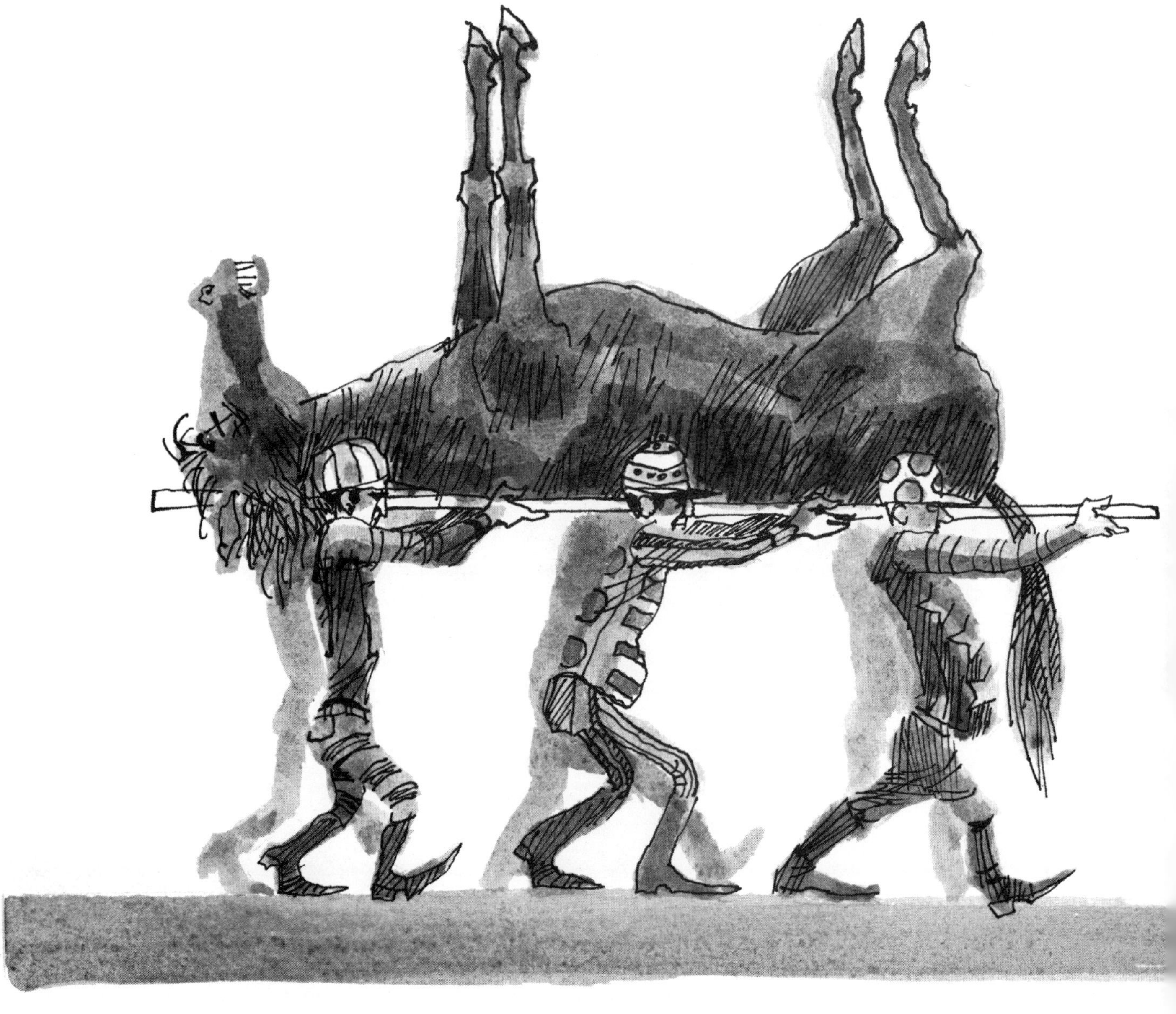

Three Legs and Heart

It was on January 18, 1928, that a seven-year-old horse known as Black Gold ran at the New Orleans Fair Grounds track. During that race, the thoroughbred stumbled, but continued to gallop until it crossed the finish line; then it collapsed in a heap. Upon examination, the astonishing discovery was made that Black Gold had a broken leg. It had run a race on three legs and heart. To end its pain and torture, a bullet was fired into the injured animal's head. Thus, tragically, ended the life of a resolute race horse.

To bestow a unique honor upon that dead race horse, it was buried in a grave dug in the infield of the race track where it had lost its life. It was the finish of the strange legend of Black Gold.

It all began with a wandering cowboy of the West named Al Hoots. He owned a horse called Useeit, and for years, man and horse wandered from county fair to county fair, winning every horse race they entered. But one day, in a claiming race, Useeit lost. When a bidder claimed the horse, Al Hoots refused to sell it. Because he had violated the code of the turf, Hoots was prohibited from taking part in further horse racing competition.

Al Hoots returned to his farm in Oklahoma, never

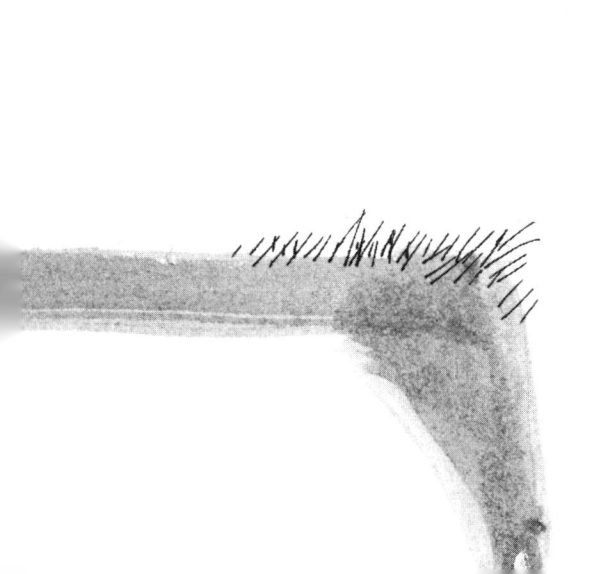

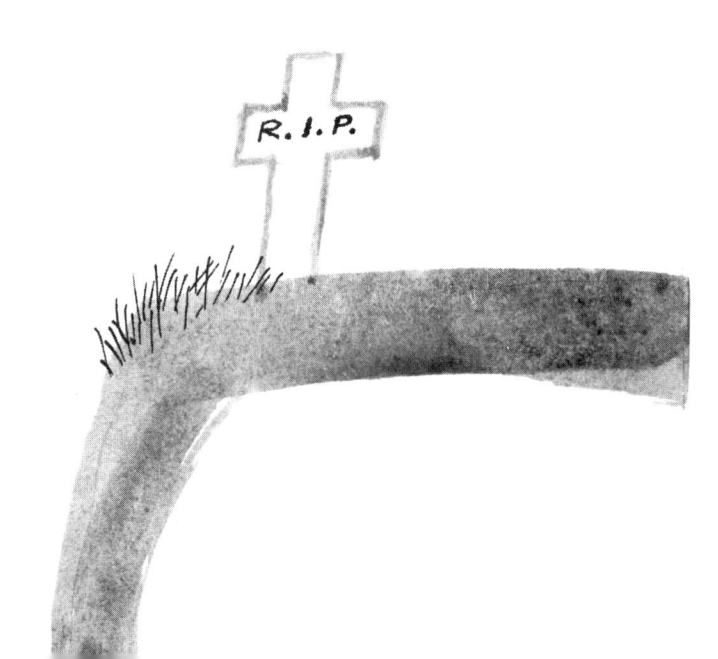

to race Useeit again. The years went by, and the unhappy cowboy became a sad and lonely man. But one day he resolved that his magnificent mare would not pass from the world without leaving behind some tangible remembrance of its turf greatness, so he had Useeit bred to a worthy stallion.

When Useeit's foal was born, Al Hoots was gravely ill. But before he died, he told his wife, Rosa:

"I haven't much to leave you except this grubby farm, and Useeit's foal. But promise me that you'll never part with that foal, no matter how bad things may be for you. That foal is my legacy to you. It will bring you luck and fame."

Upon her husband's death, Rosa Hoots faced a dark future. She had no money, and was saddled with a shabby little farm and a newborn horse hardly worth having. It was indeed an ugly little black horse with spindly legs. But Rosa Hoots kept her promise to her dead husband — she would not part with Useeit's foal. It wasn't long before the dead cowboy's prophecy began to come true. Oil was discovered on the broken-down farm, and Rosa Hoots became one of the richest women in America. In token of her good fortune, she named the young horse Black Gold. Then she hired a trainer, hoping that he might develop the young stallion into a race horse.

To Rosa Hoots' amazement, Black Gold became a winning race horse. On May 15, 1924, as a three-year-old thoroughbred, Black Gold achieved its greatest turf glory by winning America's most famous horse race, the Kentucky Derby.

For years, Black Gold basked in the glory that was its reward. Finally, when the stallion was seven years old, owner Rosa Hoots decided that it was time to retire Black Gold to greener and more peaceful pastures, far from the roar of the crowd. But she decided to see Black Gold run just one more turf competition.

On January 18, 1928, Black Gold ran the final race of his glorious turf career, and it cost him his life. But it was his most heroic gallop — since he ran that tragic race on three legs and heart.

The Wrong-Way Pep Talk

Fielding ("Hurry Up") Yost was one of the foremost college football coaches of all time. At the University of Michigan he fashioned a 40-year career that made him famous as a genius of the gridiron. His point-a-minute football teams will never be forgotten. His 1901 undefeated Wolverine eleven rolled up in that single football season an unbelievable total of 550 points to nothing for the opposition. And his 1925 Wolverine outfit, quarterbacked by All-America Benny Friedman, was perhaps the topmost team ever turned out for intercollegiate football play.

Hurry Up Yost was also an incomparable master at locker-room oratory. His fiery pep talks were legendary, inspiring his players to astonishing feats and a host of gridiron victories. However, the most unforgettable pep talk Yost ever delivered was a "wrong-way" kind which lost a championship for his team.

Late one season, some minutes before the start of an important game which was to decide not only a "Big Ten" championship title, but also a national college football championship, coach Yost launched a feverish plea to his players. It was such a masterful pep talk that he had his audience almost hypnotized. Finally, he reached the climax of his fiery oration by roaring at his mesmerized players: "Men of Michigan! Now is the time to go out that door to victory!"

With that, Yost pointed to the door for his players to exit. They jumped to their feet, and with an animal roar stampeded through it. Unfortunately, it was the door leading to the swimming pool!

Before the startled players could realize their mistake, they tumbled into the swimming pool. Some of them almost drowned before they were fished out.

Coach "Hurry-Up" Yost's wrong-way pep talk was a disaster. The drenched Wolverine players never fully recovered from their sudden ducking in the swimming pool. They lost that football game and the gridiron championship.

A Gridiron Massacre

On October 7, in the 1916 college football season, a Georgia Tech eleven entertained the football team from Cumberland College of Lebanon, Tennessee. Cumberland, a potent force in small-college football competition, had come to Atlanta to battle the Yellow Jackets of Georgia Tech, pick up a guarantee of five hundred dollars and perhaps gain some gridiron glory. But the team never expected the catastrophe that engulfed it that sunny afternoon.

Georgia Tech, then coached by the famous John

Heisman, known as the "Father of the Forward Pass," was expected to roar through an undefeated season to a national football championship. Hence, the powerful Yellow Jackets played no favorites with any of its opponents.

Georgia Tech won the toss and elected to kick off to start the football game. On the first play from scrimmage, the Cumberland quarterback was knocked unconscious, and by way of a fumble, the Yellow Jackets gained possession of the ball. They scored a touchdown on their first play.

Thereafter, Georgia Tech began to pour it on. Touchdowns were scored with bewildering speed. By the end of the first quarter of play, the score was 65 for Georgia Tech, 0 for Cumberland College. The half ended with the score at 126 to 0.

And still the Georgia Tech team wasn't fully satisfied. It continued to play with devastating power, and the score mounted higher and higher. Finally, after only 45 minutes of play, to save the exhausted and battered Cumberland team from total annihilation, the game was mercifully brought to an end. By then, the score had reached an unbelievable total, 220 to 0!

To this day, Georgia Tech's victory over Cumberland College remains the highest score ever compiled in one football game of intercollegiate competition. And so it may remain — as the supreme gridiron "massacre" of all time!

A Castoff's Farewell

Hugh Casey was past 26 when he joined the former Brooklyn Dodgers and established himself as one of the best relief pitchers in the majors. He was a player who found his trade a joyous lark in the eight happy years he was a "fireman" for the Dodgers.

He achieved the pinnacle of his fame in 1947, when the Dodgers won the pennant and clashed with the New York Yankees in the World Series. Hugh Casey played a dominant role in that classic. In the seven games that were played, Hugh Casey appeared as a relief pitcher six times! No other relief pitcher ever appeared in one World Series as many times as that.

He emerged from that World Series as its biggest hero. The entire baseball world paid him homage. But only one season later, his fame had faded so much that the Dodgers no longer wanted him, and he was given his walking papers. It was a shocking blow for happy-go-lucky Hugh Casey. He began to brood and grow restless. Baseball was no longer any fun for him. In another year, Hugh Casey was out of the majors for good.

One day, in a dark and despondent mood at his downfall, Casey phoned his wife and told her that he had decided to end it all. While his frantic wife pleaded with him not to commit a rash act, Hugh Casey shot and killed himself.

Sweet Kiss

Did you ever hear of a race horse named Sweet Kiss?

Did you ever hear of a jockey named Frank Hayes?

The horse wasn't much of a race horse, the jockey wasn't much of a rider, but together they created one of the most memorable episodes in turf competition.

Maybe it was fate that brought Sweet Kiss and jockey Hayes together. Maybe it was old age. As a race horse, Sweet Kiss had seen her best days, and there wasn't much of glory left for her old bones. At best, maybe she had one good race left in her. As for jockey Hayes, well, he was getting old and weary, too. At 35, he had ridden in only one race and had failed to place.

And so, on June 4, 1923, Sweet Kiss and jockey Hayes were together, entered in a steeplechase event at Belmont Park. It was an unimportant feature, tossed into the main racing schedule to serve more as a novelty than anything else. It would pay the winner a measly one-thousand-dollar purse.

But for Sweet Kiss and jockey Hayes, this was the "race of a century." They **had** to win to escape total obscurity! Jockey Hayes knew that never again would he ride in the big leagues, that he didn't have much of a chance in the straight events — but in a steeplechase, well, that was different, even if he had to ride an old mare. The young jocks didn't have much on him when it came to boosting a horse over the hedges and water jumps. So believed jockey Hayes as the horses went to post that afternoon. The course was to be two miles.

The favorite was Gimme, at 8-to-5 odds. Sweet Kiss was rated at 20 to 1.

Jockey Hayes got Sweet Kiss away in a clean break. At the mile, the old mare was taking the jumps like a frisky rabbit. Gimme, the favorite, was two lengths behind. Then its jockey began to give it the whip, and Gimme responded. The two horses began to take the hurdles locked neck and neck.

It became a jockey's race. The favorite had the speed on the straight and level ground, but Hayes knew how to lift his mount over the hedges and ease the landings.

Now the last jump was ahead. The two horses went up in the air, so close together that at the peak of the leap their jockeys touched shoulder to shoulder. But Sweet Kiss came down first and was pounding for the finish line as jockey Hayes, lying on her neck, pleaded, "Come on, baby — let's show 'em we're not so old!"

It was a triumphant moment for jockey Hayes as he thundered to the finish line, while the excited crowd roared its approval. What did it matter if his heart pounded fit to burst, and there was a curious weakness in his arms? He was bringing home a winner — his first in a long time!

Sweet Kiss flashed across the finish line — a winner by two lengths. And jockey Hayes' head was still nestled on his horse's shoulder.

The race was over, and Sweet Kiss, the faded old race horse, eased to a stop — with her faded rider still hugging her velvety neck. The two has-beens had won a race together! And just once more, they both lived their brief moment of glory.

But when people came over to congratulate the jockey on his victory, Hayes remained sitting on the animal's back, staring at them with glassy lifeless eyes. Then the startling discovery was made. His heart had given out while he was coming down the homestretch.

And so it happened that a faded old race horse named Sweet Kiss won a race, but for its jockey it was a sweet kiss of death — because for the first and only time, a race horse had been stimulated to victory by a dead jockey!

Felix the Fourth

Felix Carvajal was "knee-high to a grasshopper." At about the turn of the century, he was a humble and obscure postman in Havana, Cuba. In 1904, when the Olympic Games were staged at the World's Fair in St. Louis, Missouri, that pint-sized Cuban postman suddenly became possessed with the crazy idea that he was a great runner. Fate, he maintained, had destined him to go to the Olympic Games and there win the 26-mile marathon race for the glory of Cuba! Of course, in his wild dream, he gave no consideration to the cold fact that he never had been in a competitive race, and that never in his whole life had he run a long-distance race. But being an impulsive little man, Felix Carvajal publicly announced his prospective trip to the Olympic Games, and his expected triumph there.

Unfortunately, he had no money with which to finance his expedition. To attract attention to his running skill, he ran around the public square in Havana until a crowd gathered. Then he begged for contributions. By repeated performances, the postman collected enough money for his fare to the St. Louis Olympic Games.

But he sailed by way of New Orleans, and during his brief stop there he was waylaid by gamblers who cheated him out of all his money. Broke and friendless in a strange city, Felix Carvajal was still determined to run in the Olympic marathan race, so he promptly set out to run all the way from New Orleans to St. Louis — a distance of seven hundred miles! He ran and he ran, eating whatever food he could beg from farmhouses along the way. He continued to run in a grim race against time, until he finally arrived in St. Louis, just in time for the start of the Olympic marathon race.

He came up to the starting line, worn, weary and half-starved. He was wearing heavy walking shoes, a long-sleeved shirt, and long trousers. A friendly athlete took pity on him, and with a pair of scissors snipped off the sleeves, and cut the trousers in half to make Felix look more like a runner in a track suit than an amusing freak. It was broiling hot as thirty-one long-distance runners from all over the world set off on that Olympic marathon. But only fourteen were able to finish that grueling grind of twenty-six miles and 385 yards. One of them was the postman from Cuba, Felix Carvajal, who never before had run a competitive race. Surprisingly enough, he finished in fourth place. It was an astounding performance!

Felix Carvajal is not listed in the Olympic record books as a marathon champion. But in sports memory, he is recalled as the incredible "Felix the Fourth" — the runner who ran seven hundred miles to lose an Olympic marathon race.

The First International Fist-Fight

The strangest, most hair-raising, and most scandalous ring battle ever fought for the heavyweight boxing championship of the world, occurred in the town of Boston Corners, New York, on the afternoon of October 12, 1853. It was the first international prizefight fought on American soil. What happened before and after that title match will never happen again.

Back in the bare-knuckle days of boxing, John ("Old Smoke") Morrissey, a powerful, rugged, and colorful 22-year-old fist-fighter, was known as America's first heavyweight champion. He also claimed to be the greatest heavyweight fighter in the world.

However, his claim for recognition as world's champion was disputed by the heavyweight champion of Europe, an Englishman fighting under the paradoxical ring-name of James ("Yankee") Sullivan. Yankee Sullivan came to the United States in 1853, and John Morrissey consented to fight him for undisputed possession of the world's championship. The two were matched to meet in a ring battle on the afternoon of October 12, 1853 — on a farm meadow in the peaceful and prosperous town of Boston Corners   for a purse of one thousand dollars in gold, and a side bet of five thousand dollars, winner take all.

The first international heavyweight title match stirred up widespread interest throughout the country, and more than a million dollars was wagered on the outcome. It was hailed as "the fight of the century."

Naturally, the citizens of Boston Corners were proud and happy that their beautiful town would host the world's first heavyweight championship ring battle, but little did they know what was in store for them.

A few days before the title fight was to take place, Boston Corners was invaded by shady gamblers, unsavory sports, and tough hoodlums who practically took over the town, scaring its three-man police force right out of sight. Overnight, peaceful Boston Corners became anything but that.

To while away the hours before the big fight, the invading ruffians engaged in wild and bloody brawls among themselves, and many of those shady characters amused themselves by attacking the respectable natives of the town — mugging, slugging and robbing them on the streets. Some of the hoodlums simply took possession of the town's finest homes, ignoring the complaints of their terrified inhabitants.

Finally, on the afternoon of October 12, 1853, a crowd of more than 6,000 boxing fans were present at ringside to witness James Morrissey and Yankee Sullivan battle for the world's heavyweight championship. From start to finish, it was a savage and bloody brawl. In the thirty-seventh round, Morrissey was dropped to his knees by a succession of lefts and rights, but before he could rise to his feet to continue the fight, a horde of spectators rushed into the ring and began to slug it out with all within reach, raising widespread mayhem.

Unable to clear the squared circle, the frightened referee announced a curious decision. Above the roar of the milling crowd, he proclaimed the horizontal John Morrissey to be the winner and undisputed heavyweight boxing champion of the world!

Whereupon, the supporters of James "Yankee" Sullivan went berserk. Brawls broke out everywhere, with fists, clubs, knives, and pistols used. They soon spread beyond ringside and engulfed the entire town of Boston Corners.

Many citizens fled to escape the spreading terror, or hid from the rampaging hoodlums in cellars. People were beaten, stabbed and shot. Homes were looted and set afire.

A frantic, if tardy, appeal for help was sent to Governor Horatio Seymour, who promptly dispatched a company of armed soldiers to restore order and save Boston Corners from complete destruction.

The hoodlums, gamblers and other sordid characters were driven away, but they left a shambles. For Boston Corners, it was an ugly aftermath to America's first prizefight for the heavyweight boxing championship.

Thus ended the strangest, most terrifying, and

most shameful ring battle ever held for the heavyweight crown, a contest that not only staggered a town into terror, but almost destroyed it.

Also strange and unbelievable was the postscript relating to the two men who fought that first international boxing match.

The loser, James "Yankee" Sullivan, drifted to California where, in 1856, he ran afoul of law-and-order vigilantes and was hanged.

The winner, John "Old Smoke" Morrissey, retired from the ring, still undefeated as the world's heavyweight champion, and became a prominent New York political figure. He ran for public office, and became the first prizefighter elected to the Congress of the United States, where he served two terms. At 47, he waged a strenuous campaign for the United States Senate, and was elected, but died before taking office.

The First Ladies' Day

Women were once restricted from watching baseball games played in major-league ballparks.

But in 1897, the Washington Senators decided to stage their first Ladies' Day. The club owner surmised that an invitation extended to women to see his team play, for free, would attract perhaps several hundred curious females and help spread interest in the game.

When the gates opened, surprisingly, thousands of women swooped down on the Washington ballpark. For all, the object of their presence and interest seemed to be George ("Winnie") Mercer, a handsome pitcher who had been scheduled to hurl for the Washington team on that September afternoon.

Early in the game, pitcher Winnie Mercer began to find fault with the umpire's decisions on balls and strikes. The female contingent loudly sided with Winnie Mercer, against the umpire, Bill Carpenter.

In the fifth inning, Winnie Mercer became so annoyed with Carpenter that he walked up to him and presented him with a pair of eyeglasses. The ladies shrieked with delight and roared with laughter. But umpire Carpenter was not amused, and without hesitation, he ordered the handsome pitcher out of the game!

Most of the women in the stands jumped to their feet and screeched their hatred at the umpire. He ignored their wrath, and the game proceeded without the glamorous hero, Winnie Mercer, on the mound.

But no sooner was the game over than hundreds of infuriated females poured out of the stands, shouting threats at the umpire. Whereupon the brave arbiter, who had never quailed before the fury of a male mob, now became frightened and hastened to shelter. Before he could reach the safety of the Washington clubhouse, several women pounded him with their parasols and tore his clothes. Once inside the clubhouse, Carpenter demanded that the Washington club protect him. They bolted the doors and closed the heavy window shutters as a hail of stones and bricks crashed against the structure. Many of the enraged women used their parasols to beat against the shutters. Some even found clubs with which they tried to break down the door. Another horde of angry females began to vent their rage on the ballpark. Seats were ripped out, windows broken, and railings bent. The police were called, but the women continued their rampage. They remained until dark, waiting for the umpire to come out. The frightened arbiter had to be smuggled out of the ballpark to save him from mortal injury.

Many years were to pass before any other major-league club staged a Ladies' Day in its ballpark!

OH, FUDGE!

FOO! (= KILL THE Q.!xd̄ō.! UMP!)

CUSHLAMACHREE! (WHICH MEANS MALE CHAUVINIST BLIND PIG, UP AGAINST THE BLEACHERS WALL!)

MY, BUT THEY CATCH ON QUICK

The Champion and the Fly

Washington Hall in Rochester, New York, was jammed to the rafters on the night of September 7, 1865. A chattering, excited crowd anxiously awaited the beginning of a billiards match, as pandemonium reigned outside, where thousands were storming the already-locked doors. The contest was to be between Louis Fox and John Deery, meeting to decide the undisputed championship of the world. The stake was a purse of $40,000!

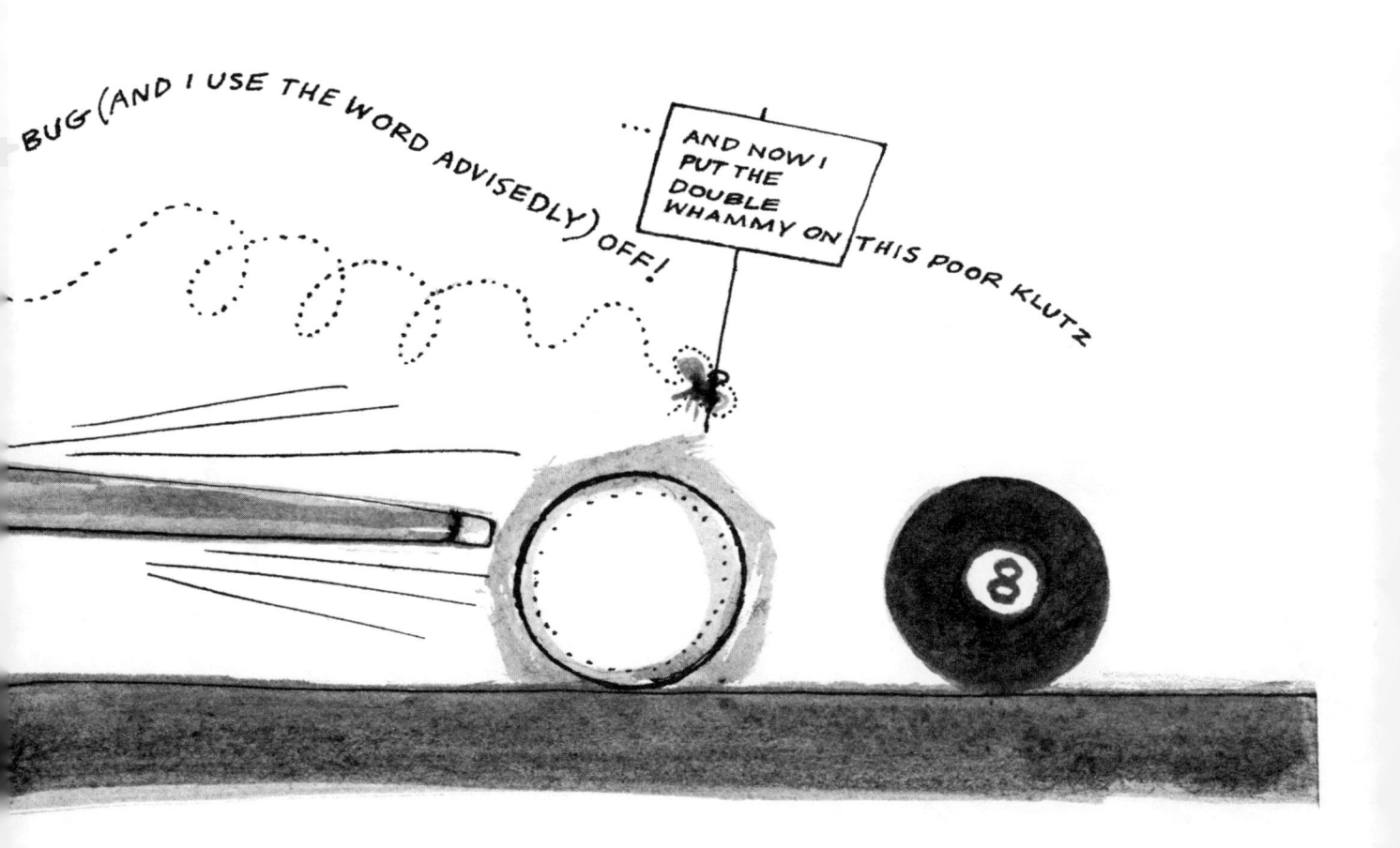

Both men were wizards with the cue. The crowd watched in strange fascination, hushed to a frozen silence. Louis Fox was at the table. He nursed the balls into position. He passed the hundred mark, then two hundred, then three hundred. His billiard cue was touched with magic. Louis Fox seemed to have complete mastery of the match. He had taken a commanding lead, and a championship and a fortune dangled at the tip of his cue.

The match was practically over. The room was heavy with tension. Only one easy shot remained for Louis Fox to win the match. The crowd, as one man, leaned forward in hushed expectancy. Fox, with a swagger, walked around the table studying the position of the balls before he made the final play to end the contest. Idly he twisted his flowing mustache. Deery, his opponent, stood gloomily off in a corner, looking like a man about to be executed.

In the frozen stillness of the ballroom, there suddenly was heard the droning buzz of a fly's wings. And out of the haze of tobacco smoke a fly appeared, circled the table, and landed squarely on top of the cue ball.

Louis Fox smiled, put down his stick, and, with his hand, shooed the fly away. Again he sighted the ivories and prepared to shoot.

The fly circled over the table, and again landed on the billiard ball. A nervous laugh rose from some spectators, then a titter ran through the audience. Louis Fox, unruffled, again put down his cue and shooed the fly away with his hand. The tittering died away. Louis Fox took up his cue and bent over the table.

The fly described an arc above Fox's head, swooped, and again settled on the cue ball. A sudden release of pent-up laughter swept through the crowd. Soon the walls reverberated with the deafening roars and high-pitched cackles of laughter.

For a second, the calm and confident Fox lost his usual aplomb. With a muttered curse, he stabbed out at the fly with billiard stick. Accidentally, he grazed the cue ball. The ball rolled aimlessly a few inches upon the green cloth. And the fly vanished.

But Fox had lost his chance to shoot, because he

had miscued by touching the ball. Now it was Deery's turn to shoot. Fox staggered back from the table and stood against the wall like a man of stone. His opponent stepped up to the table. Deery made shot after shot, playing surely and quickly, and with a remarkable run, went on to win the championship. The crowd howled with joy as the match ended.

Louis Fox looked blankly at the outstretched hand of the new champion. He could barely hear Deery saying, "Tough luck, old man, tough luck!"

Fox nodded absently, turned around, and like a man in a dream, put on his high silk hat and long opera cape and walked out into the street. People and carriages swirled around him, but Fox saw nothing but a fly circling around his head, and heard nothing but the drone of its wings and the low bubbling laughter of a crowd.

He walked and walked, faster and faster through the dark streets, to escape the sounds that filled his ears. But the laughter welled up like a Niagara roaring in his brain. And he did not stop until he came to a bridge.

Below him, waters were swirling and foaming. Fox stopped and looked down. Yes, even the waters were roaring with laughter at him. Louder and louder, nearer and nearer. And through it all, he still heard the busy drone of a little black fly.

At dawn the next day, a police boat patrolling the river found, floating in the water, the body of a man with a flowing black mustache and dressed in an opera cloak. It was Louis Fox. He had taken his life.

A common fly had not only decided the billiards championship of the world, but also the fate of the man who had lost it.

It Happened on Opening Day

Opening Day is the biggest and most exciting day of every new baseball season. Down through the years, it has been an event spiced with dignity, gaiety, music, parades and celebrities. Twice in major-league history, however, an Opening Day game couldn't be played even for nine innings — once, because of a snowball fight, and the other time, because of a mob riot.

In 1907, the former New York Giants opened their season by playing the Philadelphia Phillies. The April-day inaugural game was played in a curious setting. More than six inches of snow had fallen the night before. While the playing field had been cleared in time for the game to begin, huge mounds of snow still ringed the diamond.

That Opening Day game quickly turned into a rout for the home team. The Giants fell behind so far in the score that many of the home-town rooters became restless and unruly, and dashed out of the stands onto the field to frolic in the snow. Soon, hundreds of fans began to amuse themselves by pelting each other with snowballs. The commotion became so annoying and lasted for so long, that the angry umpire "called the game" at the end of seven innings, and forfeited it to the Phillies, by a score of 9 to 0. It was the only time an Opening Day Game ever ended with a forfeit (and because of a snowball fight!)

On April 11, 1912, curiously enough, the Giants were again involved in a disruptive Opening Day game. This time, they played against the Dodgers in the old Brooklyn ballpark. William J. Gaynor, then the Mayor of New York, was there to throw out the first ball. All started well, but by the end of the sixth inning a lopsided score of 18 to 3 was against the Dodgers.

So hundreds of home-town rooters turned ugly. They hurdled the stands and burgeoned all over the field to annoy and abuse the players. Fearful that the trouble might get out of hand at any moment, the cautious umpire "called the game" at the end of the six innings, on "account of congestion."

The sudden halt of play infuriated the crowd. In the twinkling of an eye, a full-sized riot exploded in the ballpark. Players were attacked and beaten. Hoodlums flashing knives and clubs ran wild in an orgy of violence. Even the guest of honor, the Mayor of New

York, was menaced. He was spattered with garbage, and his clothes were torn. A host of police had to club their way through the insurgents to escort him safely away from the scene.

Before the uprising was quelled, police clubs cracked hundreds of heads. Hundreds of people were injured, and many of the rioters were dispatched to jail. The Dodgers' ballpark was left a shambles.

Oddly enough, that shortest Opening Day game also served as the springboard to baseball's most enduring record — a remarkable feat that has remained unmatched to this day. The winning pitcher was the unforgettable Rube Marquard, who continued to win games until he had compiled 19 victories in a row. It became the longest winning streak ever achieved by a major-league pitcher in a single season.

When One Strike was Out

Since the beginning of big-league baseball, thousands of men have played for various teams. Of all these diamond performers, only nine were players for just one day and one game. And all of them played their game on the same day and for the same team.

It all began on the afternoon of May 15, 1912. On that day, immortal Hall-of-Famer Ty Cobb, outfielder of the Detroit Tigers and baseball's greatest player, was goaded beyond endurance by a loud-mouthed heckling fan. He lost his temper, invaded the grandstand, and before anyone could stop him, beat up his tormentor, leaving him almost unconscious. As a result of that public display of violent temper, Ty Cobb was fined one hundred dollars and suspended indefinitely by stern Ban Johnson, president of the American League.

Aroused over the penalty, Ty Cobb's teammates demanded that the severe suspension be lifted, or all would go out on strike. Their demands were ignored.

On May 18th, the Detroit Tigers were in Philadelphia and scheduled to play the Athletics, then the world's baseball champions. Hours before the start of that game, when the Detroit players learned that Ty Cobb's suspension had not been lifted, nineteen Tigers went out on strike. It was the first players' strike in baseball history.

"You've got to play!" Tigers' manager Hugh Jennings pleaded with his stubborn players. "If we don't show up for today's game, we'll not only lose it by forfeit, but the club will be fined $5,000 for failure to field a team."

But the Tigers refused to play, and some of the striking players even set up a picket line outside the ballpark.

The distressed Tiger pilot, finding himself without a team, set out on a frantic hunt for other players. He found nine Philadelphia sandlotters who had played together as a semi-pro team under the name of the Park Sparrows. They were: Aloysius Travers, Jack Coffey, Pat Meany, Hap Ward, Billy Maharg, Jim McGarr, Dan McGarvey, Bill Leinhauser, and Ed Irwin. Manager Jennings hired them to play for ten dollars each. Aloysius Travers, a young collegian studying for the priesthood, was promised twenty-five dollars to pitch for the motley sandlotters. The nine "strike-breakers" were garbed in Tiger uniforms and sent out on the field to play the tiptop team in the majors before an amused crowd of twenty-thousand spectators.

It was probably the most ludicrous "professional" game ever played. It was a farce. Although most of the players of the champion Athletics condescendingly bunted when they came to bat, nevertheless, a ground ball knocked out two teeth from the mouth of the erstwhile Tigers' third baseman, and the Detroit center fielder was knocked unconscious when a fly ball descended on his head. The fiasco finally ended by a score of 24 to 2.

The nine sandlotters who had filled in were paid off, with each receiving an extra twenty dollars for his services, and then all quickly vanished into oblivion.

The following day, May 19, was an open date for the striking Detroit Tiger team. At that time, Ty Cobb urged his teammates to play without his incomparable services. The travesty of the day before had had a sobering effect on the striking players. Most of them realized that by their mutinous action they were shaking the foundation of major-league baseball. That evening, after a heated private meeting, the Detroit players informed manager Jennings that their strike was over. Then all entrained for Washington, D.C., where the next scheduled game was against the Senators.

But the fiery-tempered Ty Cobb remained suspended for ten days, and when the Tiger players returned to their hotel, they received a notice from the iron-fisted league president, Ban Johnson, that each had been fined one hundred dollars for walking out on strike. They squawked among themselves, but paid up.

The first players' strike, brief as it was, nevertheless proved to be even more disastrous for the powerful Detroit Tigers team which had been expected to win the American League pennant. Manager Jennings was never able to straighten out his team that season, and it finished in sixth place.

The strike also furnished a unique happening in the romance of America's national pastime: an unbelievable situation in which nine unknowns of the sandlot suddenly became major-league ball players for a day, all living their most exciting hour of glory as members of the same big-league team.

The Saga of "Good-Time Charlie"

Back in 1918, with every baseball club weakened by missing players who were serving with the American Expeditionary Force in World War I, the Chicago Cubs, then managed by Fred Mitchell, found themselves starting the season without a shortstop of significant calibre. As the pennant race whirled into the month of May, the Cubs, who expected to dwell all season deep in the second division, curiously enough, suddenly found themselves within shouting distance of the first division. When the club owner got over his surprise at this miracle, he summoned manager Mitchell to his office and asked him: "What do you need to get your team into the first division?"

The manager scratched his head and slowly replied: "Well, if I had a fair shortstop, I'd say we'd have a fighting chance to finish fourth."

"All right, go out and get a shortstop!" thundered the club owner.

And so, manager Fred Mitchell sent his scouts scouring high and low for a good shortstop, but the ivory hunters returned empty-handed. By now, the Cub pilot was desperate. One morning, he burst into his office and roared: "Bring me the records on the performances of all shortstops whose names appear in the box scores of the International League, the American Association, and the Pacific Coast League." His assistants carried out his order. And for hours, the desperate Chicago manager searched through that stack of records, searching for a shortstop. At last, tired, worn, and sleepy, he finally stumbled upon the name of Charlie Hollocher, an infielder of the Coast League. Mitchell had never heard of that obscure minor-leaguer, but he ached to get to bed. He yawned, brushed all the records to the floor and snapped: "All right, get me that fellow, Charlie Hollocher."

And so Charlie Hollocher was bought for a pittance of four thousand bucks and brought to Chicago to play shortstop. But the unknown tyro proved to be a gold mine. He became a $400,000 ballplayer, a hitting and fielding sensation. Almost single-handed, Charlie Hollocher won game after game . . . and with Charlie Hollocher playing shortstop, the Chicago Cubs won the National League pennant!

"Good Time Charlie" became baseball's man of the hour! Fame, honors, wealth — all were his for the taking. No ballplayer could have asked for more. But then the strangest of all things happened. Young, strong, capable, Charlie Hollocher suddenly came to believe that playing ball was ruining his health. The club doctors examined him and found him in perfect condition. The manager took him to eminent doctors.

They, too, examined him, and unanimously agreed that he was one of the finest specimens of a healthy athlete. But Charlie Hollocher kept insisting that he was a sick man. "I can't go on playing ball any more," he said. "My health means more to me than fame. I don't want to die before my time. I'm not going to be a victim of sudden death!"

And no one could change his mind. At the height of his momentous career, Charlie Hollocher disappeared from the baseball scene. Months later, he was found living on a farm in Missouri. He refused to return to play professional baseball, even for a fabulous salary. He never came back to the game, and soon disappeared from sight and memory. But twenty years later, with bitter irony, fate finished the strange story of ballplayer Charlie Hollocher. He was found mysteriously shot to death on a St. Louis street.

Calling it Quits

Down through the years, many ballplayers have made a spectacular entrance to fame and fortune at spring training camp. For one player, however, it served as a stage for the most dramatic exit from baseball. The player who starred in that strange departure was Charles ("Chick") Stahl.

He first appeared in the Boston Red Sox training camp in the spring of 1897, a happy-go-lucky youngster out of Indiana with stardust in his laughing eyes. A sensational rookie, he also became "the life of the training camp."

It wasn't surprising that Chick Stahl became a star outfielder in his first season. He wound up with a spectacular batting average of .359. It was only the beginning of a glorious career. He became one of the game's greats, so famous and respected a ballplayer that in his tenth season he was awarded an honor coveted most by all big-league players. He was appointed manager, thus becoming both player and pilot of the Boston Red Sox. That was in 1906.

But with his elevation to manager, a curious change came over outfielder Chick Stahl. Where before he had been a gay, gabby, and friendly ballplayer, he now turned silent, moody, often brooding, and most always worrying about his team.

In the spring of 1907, when Chick Stahl met his teammates at the club's training camp at West Baden, Indiana, he seemed to be more concerned than ever. He rarely had a smile or a cheerful word for any of the players. Then, one day in March, he startled the Boston club owner with a sudden resignation as manager of the team. Never before had a major-league pilot quit during spring training. The baseball world buzzed with the news.

The surprised owner, however, simply refused to accept Chick Stahl's resignation. He persuaded him to continue as manager.

With a heavy heart, Chick Stahl most reluctantly returned to the spring training grind. For several days thereafter, nothing more was said about it. The Boston players went through their motions, while player-manager Stahl mostly kept to himself. Then, on March 28th, he made an irrevocable decision to quit. He went up to his hotel room, locked himself in, and swallowed four ounces of carbolic acid. He was only 34 when he took his own life.

No one ever made a more shocking exit from baseball, apparently simply because he didn't want to be a major-league manager!

The Olympic Champion Was an Impostor

The most unbelievable hoax ever perpetrated in track-and-field history occurred in the 1904 Olympic Games, held during the World's Fair, in St. Louis, Missouri.

The most picturesque event of that international

athletic carnival was the marathon race of 26 miles and 385 yards, running a course from the Olympic Stadium, out about twelve miles into the country, and then back to the finish line in the stadium. The day of the marathon, August 30, was blistering hot, with the temperature close to 100 degrees. Nevertheless, thirty-one long-distance runners from all over the world started. One of them, Fred Lorz, from the Mohawk Athletic Club, represented the United States.

The start was sheer chaos. Riders on horseback galloped off in front of the runners to clear the course. Some trainers on bicycles pedaled beside the runners to give them encouragement and advice. And doctors in automobiles rode behind the runners to provide medical aid if any of them needed it. The course was so jammed with vehicles that the runners had to dodge them constantly to continue running, and so dense were the dust clouds that most of the runners could not be seen.

Fred Lorz jumped into an early lead, and he held it comfortably for the first ten miles of the race. By then, the broiling heat of the day had caused many of the runners to collapse, until only fourteen remained in the race.

At the halfway mark, the fast pace, combined with the oppressive heat of the day, and a sudden seizure of painful cramps, forced Fred Lorz to retire from the race. Utterly exhausted, he dragged himself to the side of the course and watched the other runners as they passed him.

After a comforting rest, Fred Lorz accepted a ride offered him by one of the chugging automobiles cruising along the course. Thus, comfortably seated in the auto, good-natured Fred Lorz continued in that fashion, overtaking and passing all the runners still in the race, smiling and waving at them, and shouting encouragement at them as he rode by. It was no secret that Fred Lorz had quit the race.

But about five miles from the Olympic Stadium, the car which had given him a lift broke down. Refreshed by his ride and in good spirits, Fred Lorz hopped out of the car. Then, merely to keep his muscles from stiffening, he began to run again, toward the Olympic Stadium and the finish line. He made short work of it, and trotted into the stadium far ahead of the other contestants.

Naturally, as soon as he crossed the finish line, he was immediately acclaimed by the waiting crowd as the winner. Olympic officials bustled around to crown him as an Olympic champion, and President Theodore Roosevelt's daughter was about to present him with the championship cup.

Fred Lorz, a blithe spirit, knew that he was ineligible, and that the victory reception accorded him was ridiculous, but he found the entire wild and joyous situation so amusing, he decided to "go along."

While the Olympic gold medal ceremony was under way, somebody called an indignant halt to the proceedings with the charge that Fred Lorz was an imposter and a fraud, and that the real winner of the marathon was still somewhere in the distance. Pandemonium erupted in the Olympic Stadium. Fred Lorz barely escaped from the anger of the embarrassed officials and the fury of the mob he had fooled with what he thought was a glorious joke.

For his unbelievable hoax in the 1904 Olympic Games, Fred Lorz was subsequently banned from all amateur track competition for life.

"Mama's Boy"

Back in the Roaring Twenties a sensational fist-fighter known as Young Stribling appeared on the boxing scene. William Lawrence Stribling, the son of a couple of circus performers, was an incredibly handsome, well-conditioned youngster of 16 when he began fighting for fame and fortune. He was managed by his father and trained by his mother, who supervised everything he did inside and outside the prize ring. He became known as the "Mama's Boy" of the prize-ring. Indeed, to all, Young Stribling was the All-American boy.

Willie Stribling's greatest ambition as a pugilist was to win a world's ring title — and before he was twenty years old, he was a famous headliner fighting for big purses. He fought in every boxing division, from bantam to heavyweight, but was outstanding as a light-heavyweight.

The day came when "Mama's Boy" was given a crack at the world's light-heavyweight championship. The crafty boring master, Mike McTigue was the world champion — and he had agreed to defend his title against Young Stribling in, of all places, Stribling's own home town — Columbus, Georgia. The whole state simply went wild with excitement.

A frenzied crowd turned out for that bout on October 4, 1923, to see their native son win the light-heavyweight crown.

Although Young Stribling fought hard and well, Mike McTigue boxed his ears off, winning every round. At the finish of the ring battle, however, the referee made an outrageous decision. He declared Young Stribling the winner and new world's light-heavyweight champion!

An hour later, though, when the referee was aboard a train and out of Georgia, he reversed his outrageous decision and publicly declared the fight between McTigue and Stribling to be a draw. Mike McTigue was still the world's light-heavyweight champion. The referee's excuse for his original decision in Stribling's favor was that he had been fearful to do otherwise, thinking that the wildly partisan crowd at ringside might do him bodily harm.

So, after being light-heavyweight champion for only one hour, Stribling found himself without the title. His was the shortest reign a light-heavyweight champion ever had!

Willie Stribling, the "Mama's Boy," never did win a world's ring title during his flamboyant career. Life ended for him at the age of 29 when he was tragically killed riding a motorcycle on October 2, 1933.

The No-Hit Game That Didn't Count

Hurling a no-hit game is always a high spot of fame for a major-league pitcher. Only about 150 hurlers have achieved that exploit. But only one ever pitched a no-hit no-run game on Opening Day. He was unforgettable Hall-of-Famer Bob Feller, who did it in 1940.

Actually, 31 years before, Leon ("Red") Ames was the very first pitcher to hurl a nine-inning no-hit game on the opening day of a new baseball season, but it didn't count! It brought him no fame. Instead, it became the unhappiest day of his long career.

In his time, Red Ames was one of the game's greatest. He starred in the majors for 18 years. At the outset of the 1909 season, Red Ames was given the honor of pitching the inaugural game for the old New York Giants.

THIS WON'T HURT A BIT, 'OL' BUDDY......

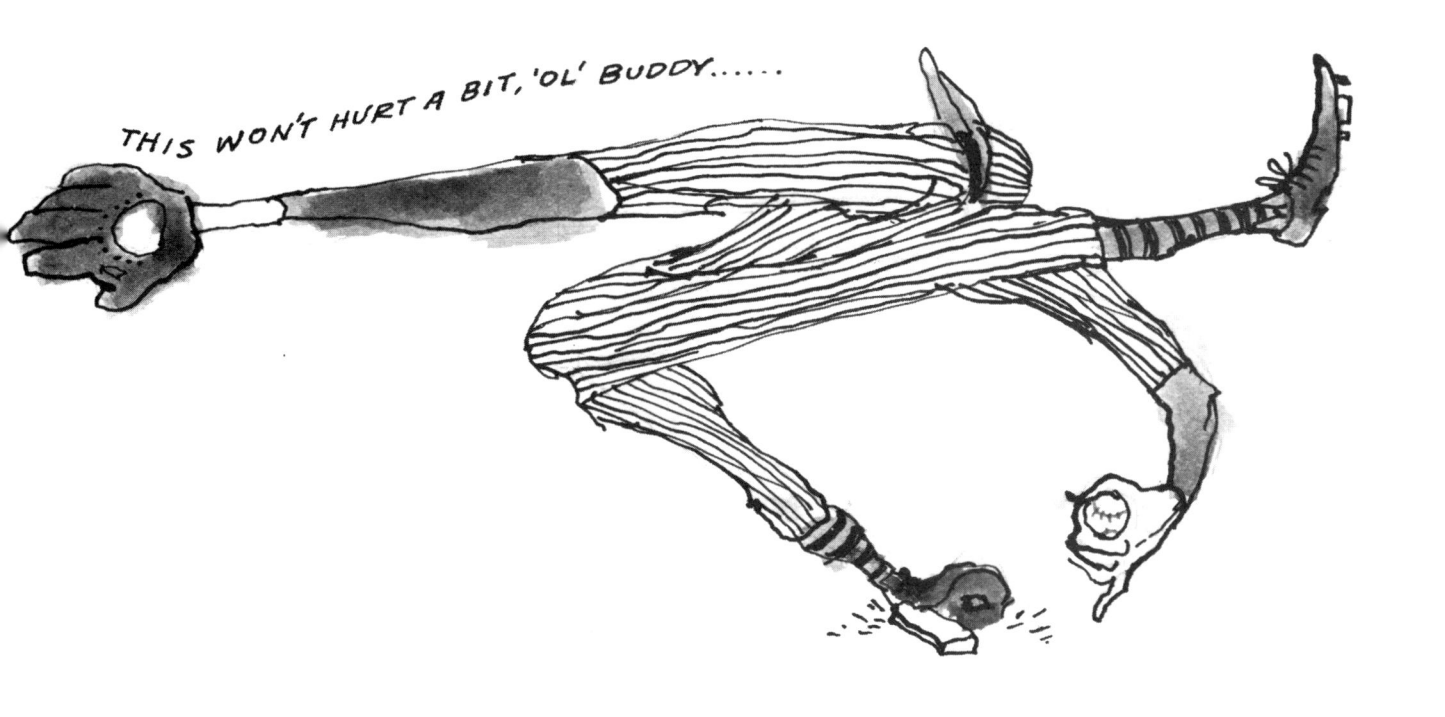

It was a proud and happy pitcher who came out to the mound. And Red Ames, a 22-game winner of the season before, was magnificent! He rose to such virtuoso heights that he awed the packed ballpark into a strange silence. Inning after inning, he set down batter after batter without a hit! It seemed unbelievable — but it was happening for the first time. Red Ames was actually pitching the first no-hit no-run game on an Opening Day. He pitched nine full innings without giving up a hit or a run!

But, surprisingly, instead of emerging with glory, Red Ames came out of that "curtain-raiser" game as the saddest of pitchers!

For, while he had pitched nine complete innings of no-hit no-run ball, his teammates had failed to help him achieve the pitching masterpiece. In those nine innings, the Giants had failed to score even a single run, so the game went into extra innings — and finally Red Ames lost it in the 13th by a shutout!

An Unforgettable Thanksgiving Day

In the summer of 1908, when the Olympic Games were held in London, a prohibitive favorite to win the grueling marathon was Italy's Pietro Dorando, then the world's foremost long-distance runner. But when he ran in that Olympic marathon and was far in the lead — just as he came within sight of the finish line, a sure winner — "Dorando the Great" suddenly collapsed.

Somehow, several muddled British Olympic officials and some zealous Italian patriots rushed onto the track, picked up the fallen runner, and dragged him across the finish line. A few seconds later, Johnny Hayes, an unknown 18-year-old American, finished the race of 26 miles and 385 yards under his own steam.

Naturally, Johnny Hayes was declared the official winner. He was the first American ever to win an Olympic marathon.

Johnny Hayes' Olympic victory, and the surprising defeat of "Dorando the Great," created controversy on two continents. So compelling was the clamor for the two runners to meet again in a foot race that an enterprising promoter persuaded Dorando and Hayes to turn professional and engage in an international competition to decide just who was the world's greatest long-distance runner.

Their first pro marathon race was set for the night of Thanksgiving Day, 1908, to be run indoors in New York's old Madison Square Garden. The 15,000 seats available were gobbled up on the first day of sale, several weeks before the date of the big event.

Hours before the start of that race, almost 100,000 people showed up at the arena in search of tickets that couldn't be obtained at any price. In a frenzy to gain admission, they pushed, fought and screamed. Hundreds of policemen tried vainly to control a wild mob that seemed bent only on defying law and order. Thousands were trampled, hundreds were injured, and billies cracked many heads. Police wagons carted off many to jail. Property damage ran high, and blood oozed freely on the streets.

Meanwhile, inside Madison Square Garden, bedlam also reigned. Police had their hands full maintaining order between the Italian rooters cheering "Dorando the Great" and the Irish rooters acclaiming Johnny Hayes. Hundreds of fist fights erupted throughout the arena.

Finally, the marathon race started, and it turned into a farce. "Dorando the Great" ran Johnny Hayes into the boards, and won by a couple of miles. On that note ended a most violent and terrifying day, a day that came, ironically enough, on Thanksgiving Day!

A Heaven-to-Earth Catch of a Baseball

Early in 1916, when all the big-league baseball players were in spring training camps to play themselves into shape for the coming season, a well-known manager attempted an incredible feat to win a large wager he had made with his players. It was to catch a baseball coming from a height never batted or thrown by man.

52-year-old, 68-inch, 300-pound Wilbert Robinson, who in his youth had been a famous major-league catcher, was the manager of the old Brooklyn Dodgers, then famed as the "Daffy Dodgers." The team was composed of the greatest collection of clowns, screwballs, and zany kooks ever assembled to play baseball at one and the same time. And Wilbert Robinson was the most eccentric and most comical manager.

Since pilot Wilbert Robinson constantly kept reminding his "Daffy Dodgers" what an outstanding catcher he had been in his playing years, there came a day when some of his clowning players inveigled him into a large wager that he couldn't catch a baseball thrown down from a plane flying high in the sky. Manager Wilbert Robinson accepted the challenge eagerly and confidently. He bet every player on his team who was willing to wager on the "impossible catch."

The next day, Ruth Law, one of the first women flyers in America, who was then doing daring stunt flying in Florida, was hired to fly her plane over the Dodgers' spring training field. The Dodger player who had been chosen to go up in Ruth Law's plane and toss out the baseball was Casey Stengel, then a well-known diamond clown.

When the moment came for the "heaven-to-earth catch" by manager Wilbert Robinson, Casey Stengel played a prank on his unsuspecting manager that almost killed him. Instead of tossing out a baseball, clowning Casey substituted a large grapefruit! The grapefruit came hurling down like a cannonball, slipped through Wilbert Robinson's outstretched hands, crashed into his chest, knocked him flat on the ground, broke, and sprayed him with juice from head to foot.

"Geez, I'm dying!" screamed Wilbert Robinson. "Boys, the ball split my chest open! I'm bleeding to death!" He wailed with his eyes shut, and his trembling hands clutched his clothes drenched with juice.

Meanwhile, the Dodger players assembled at the scene were having hysterical laughing convulsions.

Later, when eccentric Wilbert Robinson discovered that he was uninjured and that he had been the victim of a crazy prank, he actually fetched his favorite hunting rifle and went gunning for Casey Stengel, perpetrator of baseball's most hilarious practical joke.

For days thereafter, clowning Casey wisely stayed out of sight to avoid his angry manager, until he had cooled off.

The Football Game That Caused a Gun Duel

No matter how many football games are played each season, and no matter how top-notch are the teams of every gridiron campaign, the most glamorous college football game has long been the traditional game played between the cadets of West Point and the midshipmen of Annapolis.

Army-Navy football games have been bitterly contested ever since this service series was inaugurated in 1890. But the most unforgettable game of this annual classic was played in 1893. It was the only football game that ever caused a gun duel.

On November 27, 1893, a weak Navy football team took the field in Annapolis to battle against a powerful, undefeated Army team. West Point was an overwhelming favorite to win the contest with ease.

That game, however, developed into the fiercest and most savage gridiron brawl ever staged by the two service academies. From the opening whistle, the players of both teams completely forgot that they were supposed to be "gentlemen officers" as they roughed up and slugged each other at every opportunity. The game degenerated into a small-scale war between the cadets and the midshipmen. Players fell with broken bones and cracked heads. (None of them wore helmets at the time.)

The rowdyism on the football field even spread to the stands, as bitter arguments and brawls broke out among the spectators. Before the wild game ended with a surprising upset victory for Navy by a score of 6-4, it reached an unbelievable climax. An elderly retired brigadier general of the United States Army, and an equally elderly retired rear admiral of the United States Navy, became embroiled in a quarrel over the merits and sportsmanship of their respective teams. They not only wound up throwing aimless punches at each other, but challenged each other to a shoot-out — a duel on the field of honor.

No sooner had that Army-Navy football game ended than the two distinguished military officers, with their seconds, moved to a nearby isolated field to engage in their pistol duel.

Both officers had fortified their courage with several strong drinks of whiskey, and were a bit tipsy, so their aim was extremely poor, even though the distance was set at only twenty paces. Each man fired one shot at the other, and missed his target by several yards. When the shooting was over, the two duelists soon became aware of their lucky escape from sudden death.

The brigadier general and rear admiral shook hands, then happily departed from the field of honor arm-in-arm.

When news of the Army-Navy fracas and the ludicrous gun duel that was fought over it by two high-ranking military officers reached President Grover Cleveland, it so infuriated him that he promptly issued an order prohibiting the annual Army-Navy football game from taking place — for all time.

The Presidential decree banning the game "for all time" lasted only for five years, however. A new President revoked the ban, and the Army-Navy football game was resumed. Ever since then, this yearly encounter has been the most glamorous one of the college football season. But never again was there a football game played that precipitated a pistol duel.

Doomed Men of Glory

Time has woven strange and unhappy stories around many World Series heroes. Weird as the truth may be, many of them have wound up as doomed men of glory!

The first World Series hero was the immortal Christy Mathewson. In the 1905 World Series, he pitched and won three games — all by shutouts. The fabulous "Big Six" of the pitching mound died before his time, a victim of tuberculosis.

The next eminent World Series hero was a third baseman named George Rohe. He was an unexpected hero, for when the 1906 classic started, he was just an obscure utility infielder for the Chicago White Sox. But when it ended, George Rohe was the glory-boy. Only a few years later, however, as a washed-up, unwanted ballplayers toiling in the obscurity of bush-league teams, George Rohe mysteriously disappeared and was never heard of again!

In the 1907 World Series, another unexpected hero emerged. He was Claude Rossman, a utility first baseman for the Detroit Tigers. Claude Rossman was the classic's most shining hero, and the batting champion, too! But some years later, Claude Rossman died in an insane asylum.

"From Tinker to Evers to Chance" — who can ever forget the legend of that baseball trio? Not once, but four times, they won laurels as World Series heroes. But advancing time was not kind to these men. Little Johnny Evers was imprisoned in a wheelchair for many years before a merciful death ended his agony. Joe Tinker lost all his money, lost two wives, and lost a leg before death wrote finish to his story. And Frank Chance, the giant first baseman, once the strongest man in baseball, finished up as a human skeleton of less than 90 pounds before tuberculosis finally snuffed out his life and ended his misery and torture.

The brightest hero of the 1913 World Series was a hulking giant named Larry McLean. He not only emerged from that classic as a great catcher, but also as the batting champion. But as a World Series hero, he, too, was doomed to an unlikely fate. Some years later, Larry McLean was killed in a barroom brawl.

The hero of the 1918 World Series was Charley Hollocher, shortstop for the Chicago Cubs. He became baseball's "man of the hour," and after the Series, the baseball world was his oyster. But with baseball fame and fortune his for the taking, Charley Hollocher suddenly deserted the game to protect his health, so he claimed. Ironically enough, years later, he was found on a deserted street — mysteriously murdered!

The hero of the 1919 World Series, judging by all records, was a White Sox outfielder who led both teams in hitting with a healthy .375 average, who hit the only home run of the Series, who handled 30 chances in the outfield without an error, who threw out five men at home plate, and who made 12 hits. Yet, because of his role in that World Series, he was banished from organized baseball for the rest of his life! He was the tragic "Shoeless" Joe Jackson — banished from baseball because he was accused of conspiring with some of his teammates to "throw" that World Series for gambling profits.

There never was a more dramatic hero than Grover Cleveland Alexander. In the 1926 World Series grizzled old Pete Alexander fashioned imperishable history when he struck out Tony Lazzeri with the bases full to win the classic for the St. Louis Cardinals. But fate also doomed Alexander the Great to a tragic end. The last years of his life were spent in misery as he wandered the earth — neglected, forgotten, and broke. For a time, he even displayed himself as a "freak" in a penny-arcade sideshow. Finally, he died a victim of cancer.

The brightest hero of the 1936 World Series was Jake Powell. Playing for the star-studded Yankees, this utility outfielder emerged as the hero and batting champion of that Series. But years later, he killed himself!

"Iron Horse" Lou Gehrig, the immortal Yankee first baseman, was also once a World Series hero. He wound up a wasted, paralyzed, pathetic man — victim of a dread disease that snuffed out his life at 38.

Babe Ruth was a World Series hero in several classics. He, too, died before his time — a tragic victim of cancer.

Hugh Casey, one of the greatest relief pitchers in history, was also a World Series hero. In the 1947 classic he pitched in six of the seven games played by the Brooklyn Dodgers — a record that still stands! He also holds a record of winning a World Series game with one pitch. Some years later, he shot and killed himself.

World Series heroes! Their glory is brief, although their names may linger long in memory.